EXPERT
RESILIENCE

HOW ENTREPRENEURS ARE LEADING THE FUTURE IN MIND, MASTERY, AND MEANING

— Written by —

Rob Kosberg • Joel Erway • Greg Mohr • Joan Walsh • Edward C. Hill
Laura Temin • Albee Shanefelter • Selina Delangre • Jess Hughes
Rami Donahoe • Stephen Krempl • Angela Leapua • Dr. Marcia Hunter
Amir Baluch, MD • Dr. Gena Lester • Roger Khoury • Dr. Deanne De Vries
Tom Wall, PhD • Nichole Lewis • Lori Polep • Dr. Vladimir Frias

Published by Best Seller Publishing®, St. Augustine, FL
Best Seller Publishing® is a registered trademark.
Printed in the United States of America.
ISBN: 978-1-959840-50-3

For more information, please write:
Best Seller Publishing®
53 Marine Street
St. Augustine, FL 32084
or call 1 (626) 765-9750

Visit us online at:
www.BestSellerPublishing.org

For more information regarding our authors,
please visit bestsellerpublishing.org/2023anthology!

TABLE OF CONTENTS

Preface

Momentum Never Dies

(Unless You Choose to Allow It To)

by Joel Erway

Back in 2018, we were going through a very difficult time at a consulting agency I was building. We had recently brought on a bunch of clients and raised our fees. But we didn't really have our systems and processes dialed in — which would have helped us fulfill all of these clients' goals. We found ourselves training brand-new team members during a growth phase which was becoming more and more hectic.

I remember hiring a chief operating officer (COO) at the time for something like $140,000 a year. On top of that, our CEO wanted to switch our operating systems to other tools that we didn't currently have. So, we also hired a consultant to help us implement that. As we were onboarding full-time team members, our expenses increased dramatically, very quickly.

I thought it was going to be fine. I mean, we had just brought a bunch of new clients into our services. Right? Well, turns out, hiring the COO did not work out. To make matters worse, we ended up struggling with a few of our new clients who were paying us $15,000–$40,000.

It all came to a head one day, when it became evident that the process we'd built and were attempting to execute — the path we'd set — frankly, was not going to work. And so I had two choices in front of me:

1. Keep working with those clients, and keep paying the team to work toward fixing the situation.

2. Hit a reset button and refund all of those clients' fees so they would be happy and we wouldn't look bad.

It was a really difficult decision to make. Nevertheless, we owned our mistakes. We refunded those clients' fees. And we let go of the team that I had just paid.

The cost was high. We were out the tens of thousands of dollars that we'd paid the COO. We were out the fees paid to new copywriters who had been expected to complete these projects. And to the handful of clients, the refund amount was upwards of $50,000. But it was clear that it just wasn't working out. And I still feel that I made the right choice.

After all of that, I thought long and hard about if this was truly what I wanted to build — if this was truly the right path for me. And it was so bad that I ended up going into a very deep emotional spiral, where I couldn't really see more than three inches in front of my face.

I went into a hole. I went off social media. I stopped talking to my clients. I stopped talking to my team. And I was in this hole for about two months. I remember really breaking down because I thought my enterprise was a complete failure. I thought I'd let everyone down. I thought I wasn't meant to be an entrepreneur or a business owner — regardless of how much success I'd had up until that point.

I was very close to going bankrupt — to just flat-out running out of operating capital. There weren't a lot of extra reserves available, and it was very tough. So I found myself questioning everything about my skill sets, my vision, and my direction. I remember lying in bed for days and days, going deeper and deeper.

My son was just about to turn one and a half. My wife had been working for me. I remember conversations with her and doing my best to plan for the worst-case scenario. Would we both need to return to the workplace and start working for other people? How would we continue paying for our new house? It was three or four times more expensive than our last home. It was all just coming to a head.

For two months I barely got out of bed. I couldn't fathom showing my face to the world. I'm grateful that my wife let me take that time for myself. She could tell it was what I needed to do, but after a few weeks, she asked me, "What are you doing?" She then told me, "Baby, you gotta step out of this. It's gone on for far too long." She understood what was driving this for me. "Okay, fine. You learned a valuable lesson," she said. "But this doesn't mean that you're a failure."

She was right. I finally picked myself back up. I swallowed my pride. And I started to put myself back out there again — just rebuilding, brick by brick.

FAILURE IS NOT THE END

One of the biggest lessons that I carry forward from my dark experience is that you never fail — you just learn. Failure is only an endpoint if you decide it is. It's only an endpoint if there's nowhere else to go. And the only time when there's nowhere else to go is if you quit.

So I've taken this amorphous view of what success and failure is. Yes, it sucked having to refund over $50,000. Yes, it sucked having to pay contractors and team members tens of thousands of dollars. And you know what? That's life. That's business. I chose this path.

What did I do next? I got back up. And one by one, I started taking on consulting clients again. I knew that it could be my most profitable venture yet. I didn't have to pay team members. I could focus on myself and a process that I could run well by myself. I learned from my mistakes, and I started building my financial resources back up again. Eventually, after lessons learned, momentum started picking up again. And I could clearly see that the only time momentum dies is if I quit — if I stop.

I learned my lesson of resilience the hard way. Yes, I've still faced challenges since then. Yes, there were more lessons to be learned. But the biggest lesson of all for me continued to be about keeping the momentum moving forward.

No matter how difficult it is. No matter how painful it is. No matter how embarrassing it is. No matter how much shame can be felt. Resilience is about keeping everything moving forward.

The universe wants you to succeed. It might not be success in the way you envision it. But failure only comes when you quit. Failure only comes when there's an endpoint and you can't go anywhere further.

Humans have the ability to pivot — to change direction. So I encourage you to take a stance where there is no such thing as failure. There's only quitting. You got this. You can do this. You can learn. You can process. And you can keep going.

* ☆ ☆ ★ ☆ ☆ *

About Joel Erway

 Joel Erway, founder of The Webinar Agency, is a marketing expert on the podcasting circuit. With a bachelor of science in mechanical engineering, and after several crucial pivots in his professional journey, he now leads live workshops and training courses for experts in all kinds of industries.

Erway is a sales webinar expert and digital marketing consultant. Through The Webinar Agency, he helps small business owners, coaches, and consultants attract and convert higher numbers of customers and clients. By improving sales messages and implementing high-converting sales webinars, within the last couple of years he's enabled multiple clients to grow their businesses to seven figures.

Using his personal experience as well as interactions with a variety of professionals, Erway hosts two podcasts: *Sold with Webinars* and *Experts Unleashed*. He is also the author of *High Ticket Courses: The Fastest Way for Coaches, Consultants, and Service Providers to Make Six or Seven Figures with a New Hybrid Education Model*.

Beyond work, research, and personal development, he loves to travel, golf, and spend quality time with his family.

INTRODUCTION

BY ROB KOSBERG

Re·sil·ience, noun
1. the capacity to withstand or to recover
quickly from difficulties; toughness.
"the remarkable resilience of so many institutions"

If you're like me, then you thoroughly enjoy being an entrepreneur. The freedom, opportunities, and self-determination are my wheelhouse. Yet business is always unpredictable; its journey is full of ups and downs.

This book is about the entrepreneur's secret weapon, resilience. It forms the backbone of every successful venture and drives business innovation. Without resilience, the ability to survive in the harsh, unpredictable world of business would be nearly impossible. It is difficult to fight on when times seem dark. We must have the toughness to continue the fight!

Resilience isn't about just surviving, though; it's about adapting and thriving. Resilience pushes you to think on your feet, pivot when necessary, and stay ahead of the game. Resilience is the mother of innovation. It finds opportunities where others see obstacles.

Steve Jobs was famously fired in 1985 from Apple, the company he'd cofounded nearly a decade earlier. One of my clients actually sat on the Apple board, but that's another story. Jobs didn't let this small (LOL) setback stop him. Instead, he started two other ventures: NeXT and Pixar.

Pixar revolutionized the animation industry, while NeXT developed computer technologies that would later become integral to Apple. When Apple was on the brink of bankruptcy, guess what it did? The company rehired Jobs. His resilience and innovation breathed new life into Apple, leading to the creation of groundbreaking products like the iPod, iPhone, and iPad. Today, Apple stands as one of the world's most valuable companies, and it's all thanks to Jobs's resilience in the face of failure.

As an entrepreneur, you've demonstrated resilience. Maybe it was the time your business loan or funding was rejected. Or maybe it was the time payroll was due and you needed to scramble to make sure that your team was paid, even when perhaps you were not. It was the new offer, the pivot, and the "not accepting no" attitude.

Before Starbucks became the coffee empire we know today, Howard Schultz was rejected by over 200 investors when he tried to raise funds to open stores nationwide. He was told that his idea to sell premium coffee in a café setting was unfeasible. Undeterred, Schultz held firm to his vision and continued pitching his idea. His resilience paid off when he finally found investors who believed in his vision. Today, Starbucks operates more than 30,000 stores worldwide.

Being resilient is as close to a superpower as an entrepreneur can get. It is being undefeated in a world of risk, setbacks, and failure. I have always told my children that failure should not be seen as the endpoint but as an opportunity to improve and get back in the game stronger than before. In regard to the invention of the light bulb, Thomas Edison famously said, "I have not failed. I've just found 10,000 ways that won't work." His unwavering resilience led to the invention of a practical light bulb and the founding of General Electric, one of the largest and most successful companies in the world.

In the following stories, you will have an opportunity to be inspired for sure, but you will find much more than that. You will get to see resiliency skills in action. You will discover people who have skills like problem-solving. You'll find entrepreneurs who have developed a deep meaning in their lives. And maybe some coping strategies that you can use will be shared.

Resilience can serve as the rocket fuel that propels your businesses forward. And my hope for you is that these stories will transform ideas into action. One thing is for sure. The entrepreneur's journey is one full of grit, determination, and relentless courage. May you have those in abundance.

EXPERT
RESILIENCE

HOW ENTREPRENEURS ARE LEADING THE FUTURE IN MIND, MASTERY, AND MEANING

— Written by —

Rob Kosberg • Joel Erway • Greg Mohr • Joan Walsh • Edward C. Hill
Laura Temin • Albee Shanefelter • Selina Delangre • Jess Hughes
Rami Donahoe • Stephen Krempl • Angela Leapua • Dr. Marcia Hunter
Amir Baluch, MD • Dr. Gena Lester • Roger Khoury • Dr. Deanne De Vries
Tom Wall, PhD • Nichole Lewis • Lori Polep • Dr. Vladimir Frias

ABOUT GREG MOHR

Greg Mohr started off his work life in the restaurant industry. His first impression of franchising came straight out of high school at a fast-food restaurant chain. He later managed a 24-hour restaurant — another chain but not a franchise. Seventeen years of restaurant management flew by before he earned a degree in electrical engineering and physics and became an engineer.

Greg climbed the corporate ladder, working in the semiconductor industry for about 15 years. During this time, he earned an MBA degree, specializing in management information systems. Doing so did not speed up the pace of climbing the ladder, as he had hoped. In the meantime, inspired by many business books, including Robert Kiyosaki's *Rich Dad Poor Dad* series, Greg purchased rental properties and found that he could manage those on the side while keeping his day job.

As he loves sharing, Greg eventually found himself laid off, and it was a blessing. He saw an opportunity, and knew it was now or never. Working with a franchise consultant, Greg found a great fit after narrowing his goals and criteria. He never looked back. Today, he helps others find their way on the same path at Franchise Maven.

For more information regarding our authors,
please visit bestsellerpublishing.org/2023anthology!

CHAPTER 1:

RESILIENCE THROUGH UNSEEN OPPORTUNITIES
(DON'T JUDGE A BOOK BY ITS COVER)

BY GREG MOHR

Don't judge a book by its cover. You have all heard that before. First impressions are not always what they seem.

The big mistake many of us make is that we jump to an assumption and often walk away from great opportunities purely because we didn't take the time to research them in more depth.

When I first started looking for a franchise, I became "click happy." I started clicking on many different franchise offerings that I saw online. I received many calls from many different franchises, and it became quite overwhelming. I finally came across a couple of different franchise consultants (who knew such a thing even existed?). They were able to help me find a franchise without me spending all that time and effort going through each one myself. Well, I ran my franchise for a while, but in the back of my mind I kept thinking about what those consultants did — essentially changing people's lives for the better forever. At the time I was helping businesses save money on their telecommunications bills through my franchise. While it was very interesting, I really liked the idea of helping people like me who had no idea where to start when it came to finding franchise opportunities.

So when it comes to franchising, the "covers" most folks judge the industry by are as follows:

- All are brick and mortar
- Buying a job
- I can't afford it
- I don't have the skill set / I've never run a business

AN IGNORED BOOK

Let's take a look at Jerry as an example. Jerry worked in the tech industry for years. He would drive by other business franchises all the time, he said. He told me he'd always dreamed of owning one but knew they were out of his price range since they needed a building. He had heard they needed at least a $500K net worth and $100K liquid, which he did not have (he'd spoken with a few of them). He had talked to many business brokers but could not find any private businesses for sale that he liked. He had almost given up when we connected on LinkedIn and struck up a conversation on businesses for sale. Jerry, like many people I work with, was really getting tired of the corporate world and wanted to do something for himself. Twenty years of making money for others, having to be there from 9 to 5 every day, and getting only a couple of weeks for vacations each year was getting really old. He did not see a path where he could have more time for himself and his family and do the things he liked while doing the same thing he had been doing for another 20 years.

So let's take a look at Jerry's assumptions …

All are brick and mortar

Most of the time when I speak with people about franchising, they first think of the restaurants that everyone knows. Most people don't realize that there is a franchise in almost every industry. We see the brick-and-mortar franchises all the time. McDonald's, Taco Bell, Supercuts, Great Clips. For brick and mortar, "you build it and they will come" is the general theme. And with a great franchise that has an outstanding real estate team, they will indeed come. The brick-and-mortar franchises have to be out in front of people. You need prime real estate. This is why most of the people I speak with only think of brick-and-mortar franchises when I ask them what they know about franchises.

What we don't see are the service industry franchises. For the service industry, your clients do not necessarily know you exist until they need you. A great franchise system is needed to drive people to you when the need arises. What service industries are there? Home improvement, pest control, lawn care, senior care, restoration, tutoring, and many others.

Buying a job

I don't want to buy a job. Most folks see franchising as buying themselves a job. When I tell folks about the service industry, the first thing they tell me is that they do not want to buy a job. You can buy a job through franchising, but for the most part franchisors want you to grow the business. This means working on the business, not in it. There are also many franchises that can be run from a semi-absentee to an absentee standpoint. What does this mean?

Time-wise, for a semi-absentee franchise you are looking at 10–15 hours per week managing the manager and the profits and losses. Generally, you will be finding the manager, with the franchise's help in some cases. Some franchises can be run almost completely absentee. Franchises have the management team in place or will hire the management team for you. In this case, running it can be almost completely passive. And yes, in some cases you can run the franchise yourself.

Many people may consider this buying a job. But think about this: Can you sell your corporate job when you get tired of it for three times its earnings before interest, taxes, and amortization (EBITA)? Probably not. While you may be the only one running it, you can still, at some point, hire and train someone to do it for you. Can you do this with your job? Wouldn't that be great? Hire someone to take over your corporate job, and you take part of their pay. Ya, probably not going to happen. But it can happen with a franchise. Read on for some people's excuses or reasons they need convincing.

I can't afford it

This goes back to the preconceived notion that all franchises are brick and mortar. Brick-and-mortar franchises are the most cost intensive. This is due to the build-out needed. Generally, they start at around $250K total investment and go up from there. You will generally need about $100K liquid and $500K net worth.

Service industry franchise investments are much lower. Generally, you are looking at around $50K–$150K. The difference is, you work from home (or a small office, if needed). Yes, there are franchises that can be run from home. This does not mean clients are coming to your home; it means you go to them — either to their home or office. If you have not used their services, you have probably not heard of them.

I don't have the skill set / I've never run a business

Have you been in the corporate world, and are you a manager? Have you run a crew or team of people? Then yes, you have the skill set. You have run a business within a business. None of the above? Do you like doing things yourself and don't want employees? We have a franchise for that. Franchises are looking for people who believe in them. They can teach you the rest.

Does the franchise require a person who is good with sales? Are you good at sales? If not, then hire someone who is. What about service industries that remodel kitchens or garages or that do plumbing or electrical repair? If you don't have the skill set for installations like these, then hire someone to do it for you. Your goal is to operate the franchise, build the business, and grow the customer count. Grow revenues. If you believe in yourself and the franchise, you have the skill set. Franchises will teach you everything you need to know. And yes, they have the methods in place to help you find the people who will work in the business.

AN OPPORTUNITY FOR SERVICE (AND A GREAT BOOK READ)

Jerry and I had a few great conversations, and we went through the different franchise opportunities available. It turned out that Jerry really likes getting involved in his community. He has a passion for helping others, and we have a franchise for that. Jerry was astounded. We put him in a service industry helping others — with a total investment of around $150K. Jerry had never heard of the franchise, but that is normal for the service industry. Your clients do not know you exist until they need you.

So there it was. Jerry had assumed the book only involved franchises he could not afford, so he had practically given up on his dream. But many of his assumptions turned out to be false when he opened the book and started reading it with my help. Imagine Jerry's excitement, as he now had the opportunity to leave his very unfulfilling 9-to-5 job and finally do something he had only dreamed about: helping others, spending more time with his loved ones, and having more time for life itself.

Can you imagine getting up in the morning and looking forward to going to "work" (can you call it work if you enjoy it?). In addition, Jerry now realized that how much money he makes is determined by the amount of effort he puts into his business. No ceiling for him based on his position in the corporate world.

Jerry is now in a business he loves and has walked away from his corporate job. He is totally in control of his future and can take all the time he wants to be with family and do the things he enjoys. He is also one of the top franchisees at his new franchise. Had he not taken the time to speak with me on LinkedIn and taken a chance there may actually be something out there for him, he would not be in the great position he is in today.

So, how about you? What is holding you back from finding out more? Go to the Anthology Author Resource page or the Franchise Maven's website. There you will find the Matrix of Business types. This will give you an idea of the different types of franchise businesses available and get you thinking about the different businesses you can run.

Feel free to reach out to me at any time, and we can go over the various opportunities together.

Greg Mohr
Franchise Maven
361-772-6401

About Joan Walsh

Joan Walsh is a business coach, consultant, author, and speaker. She has served organizations and individuals in both the public and private sectors for over 30 years.

She specializes in helping businesses achieve higher levels of performance by creating plans, setting goals, and implementing actions to achieve extraordinary results and success.

Joan is a cofounder of Kashbox Coaching. She is the author of *Ready, Set, PLAN, Go! Strategies to Accelerate Your Success* and *Blazing Your Own Trail: A Guide for Women on the Way Up.* She's also the coauthor of *Coach: 10.5 Reasons to Hire One.*

For more information regarding our authors,
please visit bestsellerpublishing.org/2023anthology!

CHAPTER 2:

THE RESILIENT 21ST-CENTURY LEADER

BY JOAN WALSH

Leadership is a topic that has been with us for decades, and many continue to study it. There are conferences, seminars, workshops, books, webinars, podcasts, online courses, and more which cover the importance of leadership. Leadership is about guiding one's self, individuals, people on teams, or organizations through a focus on knowledge, skills, attitudes, behaviors, and habits. Leadership is a process that constantly changes as situations change. A specific leadership style is often defined by how you handle responsibilities, work with others, and take action to provide results.

Our country and world have changed drastically over the years. To be a leader today, one needs to know the attributes necessary to become a 21st-century leader.

I look back at my life and at those I've observed. My journey to become the leader I am today started with my parents and then continued with teachers, colleagues, mentors, self-development coaches, mastermind groups, and other leaders. Some were very good and others were not. We learn from all of them. Doing so is also an opportunity to decide if we want to be a leader or follower.

We all go through positive times (success, thriving, and happiness) and negative times (mistakes, obstacles, and challenges). It was during both kinds of times that I learned to be the best I can be. Rarely did I get it right the first time, or the tenth. I never saw negatives as downers. The key was to never give up. Success is the result of small, significant steps completed consistently over time that create a radical difference. At times, a different direction emerged from new information or stepping back and reevaluating what was not right. Over time, I learned the right direction, took action, and gained positive results.

I have been a coach for over 30 years. I have worked with C-level leaders, entrepreneurs, individuals, and teams in companies. Many clients seek to focus on goals to achieve their vision with the right people. Other companies bring me in to "fix" a situation where a person has gone off-track with their managers or teams.

Let me share with you a "fix" opportunity that went beyond everyone's expectations. Leslie was the director of finances. She had three direct reports and 30 additional team members. She reported directly to the chief financial officer. In going into this opportunity, I was told that she needed to become a leader. She was a very bright woman and achieved all her department goals, but her colleagues and team did not care for her approaches. It turned out that she thought she was right all the time and was not open to other people's recommendations. This resulted in colleagues avoiding her and a team with low morale. I was told that she had no self-awareness.

Over time, she began to see where she needed to grow. It was like a light bulb turning on in her head, so many times and ways. She went from being offensive (it was always her way) to being open to new ways of leading. She became a 21st-century leader.

A 21st-Century Leader

So, how do we lead today? What are the attributes, traits, skills, knowledge, behaviors, and habits that are necessary to become a 21st-century leader? Let's take a look at the ways to lead the self, individuals, teams, families, and communities.

We start with the leader's attitude and mindset being contagious. Confidence is power. It is an attribute that is developed and earned.

The leader seeks to be inspirational and rally people toward a common goal. They have a vision. They outline the road map for how a goal can be achieved but give their team freedom in achieving it. They challenge their team to create original ideas and solutions.

A 21st-century leader has authenticity and integrity. We are human. We communicate with feelings, not words. Twenty-first-century leaders are honest. Their yes means yes and their no means no, which results in people trusting them. When a leader doesn't stay true to their word — when they can't be trusted — it makes people reluctant to follow them. This is true in the workplace, at home, and in the community.

A 21st-century leader communicates effectively. Effectiveness is important in both verbal and nonverbal communication. Proper communication often requires a mix of verbal and nonverbal signals to convey meaning. Consider the differences between these forms of communication and how to use them.

> **Delivery:** Verbal communication can transpire over the phone, through email, in written letters, and in face-to-face or Zoom conversations. Most nonverbal communication happens only when two or more people can see each other.

> **Intentionality:** A difference between the two types of communication, verbal and nonverbal, is that the words a person chooses — verbal — tend to be intentional, whereas many elements of nonverbal communication can be unintentional or out of a person's control and can impact reception. Nonverbal communication can be unconscious; for example, a person who folds their arms and steps back shows distance, whereas a person who stands with their arms by their side shows openness.

> **Authenticity:** Nonverbal behavior like body movements, mannerisms, or physiological responses (blinking or fidgeting) can influence communication, altering the authenticity of your spoken words or causing them to take on a different meaning. Nonverbal messages

can be more powerful than verbal communication, as human bodies can subconsciously deliver messages that they are verbally not conveying — actions speak louder than words.

Engagement: Nonverbal signals are a great way to communicate attentiveness and engagement. It is not enough to verbally tell someone you are interested in what they are saying; controlling your posture and eye contact will demonstrate to others that you are interested, whereas looking around or at your phone can express lack of interest.

When you communicate with others, keep in mind that 7% is verbal, 38% is tone, and 55% is nonverbal — the visual. That means 93% is nonverbal. Awareness of nonverbal signals and tones allows you to communicate effectively with the verbal.

A 21st-century leader is humble and "knows thyself." In today's diverse workplace, emotional intelligence (EQ) makes an impact on those who are led. A leader knows that a high intelligence quotient (IQ) can get a person hired, but it will be their EQ that gets the person promoted.

EQ involves self-awareness, self-management, and relationship management. If you respond with emotion that is not appropriate, reflect on "why." You can't always control how you feel, but you can control how you act upon those feelings. If you feel yourself beginning to respond emotionally to a situation, take a pause. In that pause, ask yourself: Does this need to be said? Does it need to be said by me? Does it need to be said now? Will it change anything? If not, don't say it. If that question needs to be responded to, adjust the volume.

We know through research studies that 90% of top performers have a high EQ. The internet provides many articles and studies about the importance of emotional intelligence today.

A 21st-century leader has genuine care for others. The leader's job is to make others successful. A leader makes sure that each team member has what they need to get their work done. The leader knows that when a team succeeds, the leader succeeds. Leaders need to lead by example.

A 21st-century leader seeks the opinions of others. Leaders know they aren't always the smartest one in the room; therefore, their ego isn't bruised when someone offers a better solution. This creates great team morale. When others share a solution, everyone listens with an open mind.

Leaders know that no one should ever feel belittled. Today's leaders know that praise is done publicly, while criticism is done one-on-one.

A 21st-century leader surrounds themself with effective teams. They know they need to create a team of people who are talented and knowledgeable in ways that they may not be. A way to do this is through the interview process. During the interview, listen and observe to see if the person has a strong desire to be on the team — a hunger for the position.

It is during the onboarding process (typically the first 90 days) that you can evaluate whether you've selected the right person.

> **Step one:** Create interaction from the beginning — support and compliment the individual based on small tasks that are done correctly.
>
> **Step two:** Provide clarity and direct instructions on tasks. Let them know what they are responsible for. The more in control they feel (confidence), the better their performance will be. Let them have early wins and make them feel they are contributing.
>
> **Step three:** Let them know and understand their goals. The pace at which a new team member begins will determine the pace of their career with the team.
>
> **Step four:** Set high expectations. The more they feel a part of the team, the better they will do.

As the new team member goes through the onboarding process, it is the leader who lets them see that there are some areas in which they are more knowledgeable than the leader. A leader understands that gaining the wisdom of many people contributes to the best solutions for the whole organization.

To become a 21st-century leader, take the time to review, study, and learn the many aspects noted above — what it takes to be a leader today.

MAKE YOUR DECISION

Now let's get back to my client. Leslie worked hard to become a 21st-century leader. She looked for opportunities to lead others. She was a member of a women's organization and decided to become part of the leadership team. She blossomed and became the president of the organization. She took on challenges and resolved problems with the team. The organization grew by numbers and expanded the focus of their mission. These results were achieved because she had become a 21st-century leader and had helped others to become leaders too.

She also decided to become a board member for her home association. Prior to that, she was one who had complained about monthly dues that were going up, yet there was no change in the neighborhood. Grounds keeping of the common areas and weekly lawn care never improved. Leslie was able to improve snow removal on driveways and sidewalks, so she knew she could make a difference. She was nominated for and voted onto the board. Mind you, this was the location of her second home. She had to drive two hours to attend the meetings. Not a problem for her. Through her input during those meetings, change occurred. She first had to get her fellow board members to see what she saw. One by one, the board worked together to resolve many problems. The home association members saw the results. Instead of many complaints — even though they still got them — the association received compliments from many people.

During this time, Leslie became the chief financial officer of her company. Prior to this announcement, she prepared her replacement and restructured the department. When given the opportunity, she took it, knowing she was ready. She was welcomed to this position by her colleagues and individuals in the company.

When she told me about her new position, she wanted me to know that all of this had happened because of our working together. I made it very clear to her that she had done all the work and was open to transforming into a 21st-century leader.

So now it is your turn. Look at yourself and make the decision to become a 21st-century leader in your life — in the workplace, at home, and in your community!

About Edward C. Hill

Edward Hill is a number one international Amazon best-selling author, speaker, and business consultant. He's the CEO/founder of Prosperous Internet Marketing Inc. and Prosperous Christian LLC. He has been featured on ABC, NBC, CBS, FOX, and dozens of radio stations, as well as in international publications and podcasts. Eddy has spoken to and taught tens of thousands of small-business owners and entrepreneurs how to massively grow their businesses. He won the prestigious Speaker of the Year award, twice, from the International Awards and Personalization Association.

Through his registered trademarked P.R.O.S.P.E.R. Formula™ program, Eddy helps his clients set up specific systems to dramatically increase their prospects, increase their closing ratio, increase order average, increase sales frequency, increase productivity, decrease expenses, and increase retention. The result is guaranteed to double your net profit.

Eddy is truly passionate about helping business owners and entrepreneurs. He is on a mission to double the profits of a thousand businesses in the next five years.

Would you like your business to come along for the ride?

Take a free business assessment, worth $979. We will send you a detailed strategy plan that will maximize your profits in less than 90 days. Go to this Anthology Author Resource page or Prosperity Formula's website for more information!

CHAPTER 3

FOUR CIRCLES OF SUCCESS

(MINDSET, SKILL SET, TOOLSET, GET OFF YOUR ASSET)

BY EDWARD C. HILL

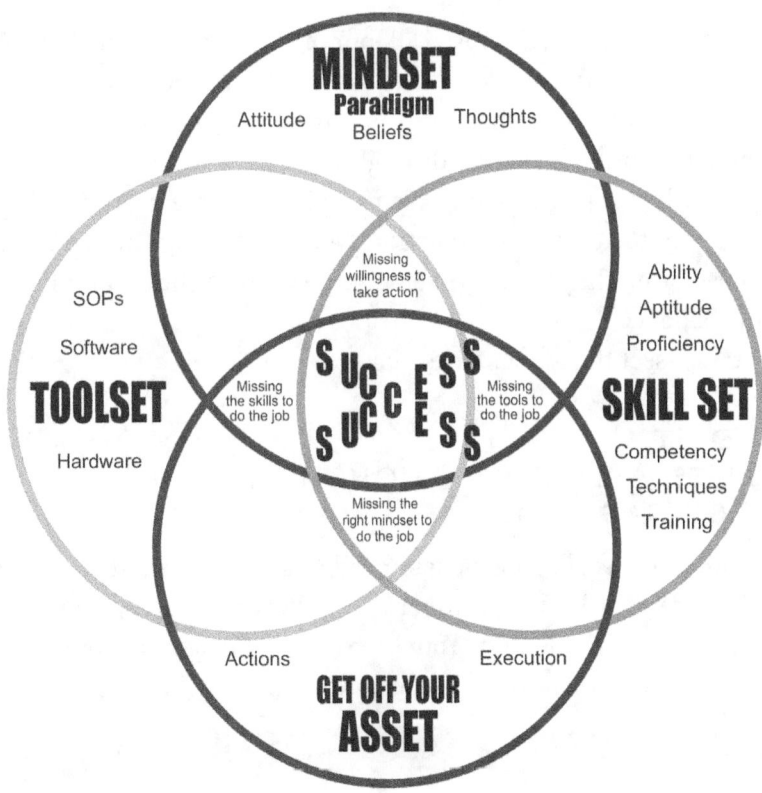

Arguably, the greatest series of movies about success and resilience is the Rocky franchise. And if you narrowed it down to just one movie, it would be *Rocky IV*. This is the movie where Rocky has the fight of his life when he takes on the formidable Soviet boxer Ivan Drago.

By all accounts, Rocky was the inferior fighter. Drago towered at 6 feet, 6 inches and weighed 261 pounds. Rocky was 5 feet, 10 inches and weighed 210 pounds.

I realize the matchup is fictional, but we can learn a lot from the writings of Sylvester Stallone. Let's reverse engineer the exact reason Rocky won (spoiler alert: sorry if you haven't seen it).

Successful people and successful businesses have something in common. In fact, they have four things in common. I call these the four circles to success: Mindset, Skill Set, Toolset, and Get Off Your Asset. Each of these circles can stand on its own, but if you combine them, they synergize and you get exponential results, and the probability of success is almost a certainty.

Both Rocky and Drago used all four of these circles to success. They both had this unequivocal mindset to win, not just for themselves but also for their country. They both had mastered the arduous skills of boxing at a world-class level through thousands of hours of practice. They both had a plethora of tools to train for success. And indisputably, they both took massive action. When all things are equal (and they never are), the winner will emerge because of one extra thing. In a word, resilience.

Let's dissect the first circle to success, mindset.

MINDSET
(BELIEFS, ATTITUDES, THOUGHTS, YOUR PARADIGM)

Your mindset is a collection of habitual thoughts and attitudes that shape your innermost beliefs. Your innermost beliefs are called your personal paradigm or your identity. Your personal paradigm is your way of looking at a situation — how you perceive it and understand it from your perspective. Your paradigm completely directs how you see yourself and the lens through which you see the world around you. It's your frame of reference that contains your basic assumptions, your innermost beliefs, your ways of thinking, and your methodology of reasoning.

> Your mind is the garden, your thoughts are the seeds.
> The harvest can either be flowers or weeds.
> — William Wordsworth

It's like the tale of the two shoe salespeople who were sent to a developing country to sell shoes. When the first one got there, he called back to the office and said, "Get me a plane ticket home. This is useless. No one wears shoes around here." The second salesperson looked around, and he called the office and said, "Send me all the shoes you have. No one has shoes around here!"

Your mindset is a psychological outlook that predetermines your interpretation of and your responses to every situation. Your identity is your beliefs, your mindset, which drives the actions that you take and the results you get. Your mindset absolutely skews reality, either positively or negatively. Rarely do we have thoughts or make decisions that come from a neutral mindset. Our preprogrammed mindset will set the tone for every situation unless we consciously change it. That's right: unlike animals, humans can consciously choose to change their mind.

We can change these automatic reactions, thoughts, and behaviors by consciously and repeatedly adjusting the way we view those stimuli and ultimately by changing our response to those stimuli. That's exactly how we choose the success mindset.

We can take a peek into Rocky's mindset — as well as Sylvester Stallone's, because he wrote the movie — by looking at the pep talk Rocky gave to his son in the movie *Rocky Balboa*.

While addressing the mean and nasty nature of the world, he said, "It ain't about how hard you hit, it's about ho hard you can get hit and keep moving forward."

Undoubtedly, Balboa and Stallone have the mindset for success.

SKILL SET
(ABILITIES, APTITUDE, COMPETENCY, TECHNIQUES, PROFICIENCY, TRAINING)

A skill is the ability to perform an activity in a competent manner. Over the years, many gurus and experts have separated out different skills into easy-to-swallow categories, like soft skills and hard skills. Soft skills are things like communication and interpersonal skills, leadership skills, and problem-solving skills; even emotional intelligence is a soft skill. Hard skills are more specific physical skills like welding, designing, juggling, bookkeeping, speaking foreign languages, playing the guitar, computer programming, and boxing.

Throughout our life, we all have mastered hundreds of skills — everything from driving to tying our shoes to making coffee to golfing (well, no one has truly mastered golfing).

In the book *Outliers*, Malcolm Gladwell contends that a person could become world class if they put in over ten thousand hours of deliberate practice. *Deliberate* is defined as purposeful and systematic practicing in such a way that it pushes your skill set, with the specific goal of improvement. Though most psychologists say this theory is way oversimplified, they all agree that hard and soft skills are a "learned" trait. No one is born with the amazing ability to hit a five iron, program an app, pick a banjo, or dodge a right hook.

Those skills must be learned through hundreds, maybe thousands, of hours of deliberate practice. The good news for you and me is, we probably don't need to be world class — just great — and you are probably already 90% of the way there. All you really need to do is solidify your direction and make some minor tweaks by adjusting your execution over and over and putting in the work.

The fastest and surest way to better your skills is by having an accountability partner or coach. You need someone who will show you the path, establish your goals with you, and hold you accountable.

In *Rocky*, Balboa was a bumbling neophyte who barely had the coordination to jump rope. By *Rocky IV*, he had undisputedly mastered the arduous skills of boxing at a world-class level, because he had amazing coaches and trainers. First, it was Mickey Goldmill, and later he was coached and trained by Apollo Creed and Tony "Duke" Evers.

Go recruit an amazing coach to help you hone your skills. A great coach will push you way beyond your personal limits as well as help you sidestep the pitfalls and show you the shortcuts to success. Do it today — "There is no tomorrow!"

TOOLSET
(HARDWARE, SOFTWARE)

To prepare for the unsanctioned World Heavyweight Championship match in Moscow on Christmas Day, Ivan Drago used high-tech, state-of-the-art equipment, a team of trainers and doctors monitoring his every movement, and regular doses of anabolic steroids. Rocky, on the other hand, went back to the basics, running in deep snow over mountainous terrain and doing workouts using antiquated farm equipment, like sawing logs, chopping wood with an axe, lifting heavy rocks, and pulling a sleigh.

In today's world, there are more opportunities than ever before. We don't need maps to show us where the gold is; we need tools to help us get to the gold. The toolset is the shovel, pickaxe, backhoe, bulldozer, and metal detector that will help make it easier and more efficient for you to dig for the gold.

Tools like software and hardware are the cheat codes to the game of success. They allow you to skip over pitfalls, defeat your foes, speed up production, leapfrog your competition, minimize waste, and maximize your most valuable asset: your time.

The dilemma is deciding which tools we should hitch our wagon to and, even more troubling, which ones we shouldn't. My advice is, success leaves clues. In your industry or your profession, there are probably thousands of phenomenally successful businesspeople who you could and should learn from. What tools do they use? What systems, processes, and software do they use? Amazingly, most successful people will happily divulge these things if you just ask. It's your job to find the right tools and then implement them.

That leads me to the last circle of success …

GET OFF YOUR ASSET
(ACTIONS, EXECUTIONS, PRODUCTIVITY)

The pinnacle question is, how do you — specifically YOU — change your behaviors and start taking consistent positive actions? Obviously, it's easier said than done. There is an excellent aphorism attributed to Dr. Henry Cloud and Dr. John Townsend that says "We change our behavior when the pain of staying the same becomes greater than the pain of changing. Consequences give us the pain that motivates us to change."

Unfortunately, most people don't want to change their behavior; they want to change the consequences of their behavior.

Most consequences are not enough to get someone to change and take a new action; they would rather keep the pain of staying the same. Even people in dire situations have only a 10% chance they'll actually change for good.

I'm a huge believer in setting daily "tactical" goals: something you can actually check off a list. For instance, I set a goal to work out 208 times a year. This equates to four days a week, on average. I don't set a goal to lose weight and get in better shape — even though I undoubtedly will — but those are not tactics I can check off. You need to be extremely specific in your daily or weekly tactics.

I further define "working out" as a 2-plus mile run, 30 minutes of heavy weight training, or 12,000 steps in a day. At the end of the day, it's a simple yes or no to the question "Did I work out?" You should do the same in setting your yearly goals by breaking them down into daily and weekly tactical achievements that you can check off a calendar.

Your focus is on the daily activity that, if done consistently, will absolutely make you successful. By using the tactical goal-planning strategy, there are only two ways you can fail: 1) you set up the wrong daily tactics, or 2) you did not execute; you did not do the daily activity that produces a result. This makes it quite easy to troubleshoot what went wrong.

It's not intellect we lack but emotional determination and strength to act. At the end of our lives, it is assured that we will be more disappointed by the things we did not do than by the things we did do. Resolve to stop wishing, stop "shoulding" all over yourself, and plan specifically what you will do each day to propel yourself forward, and then resolve to work your plan consistently. Ignite strong feelings. Get mad! Indifference is a disease that causes stagnation. Disgust and resolve are two powerful emotions that will help you act. Disgust says, "I have had it." Resolve says, "I will." Action puts fear to flight. No excuses, just action.

RESILIENCE
(RECOVERY FROM ADVERSITY)

Resilience means the ability of a person to adjust to or recover readily from adversity. Rocky won because of his stick-to-itiveness, his persistence, his drive, his vitality, his resilience! Rocky says it best: "Every champion was once a contender who refused to give up."

It is like Newton's first law: "An object in motion stays in motion with the same speed and in the same direction unless acted upon by an unbalanced force."

This is relevant to our circles of success. Once we are in motion, we can be defined by our velocity, which is speed with a direction. Then inertia takes over, which is the tendency of an object to resist changes in its velocity. The key is to get in motion. Once you are in motion you must have resilience to stay in motion. Because, just like Rocky, you are guaranteed to get hit. My absolute favorite quote from Mike Tyson is relevant here. He said, "Everyone has a plan until they get punched in the mouth." What about you? What's your plan when you get hit?

Take massive action today. Today is just tomorrow's yesterday. What are you going to do today that makes a difference in your life? What's the one thing you can do today to move you toward your goals? Whatever your answer is, do it today! The new you starts right now.

Just like Rocky, you can strategically implement the four circles of success and "keep moving forward." If you do, you'll assuredly get to scream victory at the top of your mountain. Go get 'em, tiger.

About Laura Temin

Laura Temin is more than a clinician. She is a clinician who faced her own traumas, limitations, and past programming and went from VICTIM to VICTOR.

Laura takes an integrative and holistic approach. Her work spans over twenty years and she has seen firsthand that success demands a comprehensive approach. The nine years she spent working in the Emergency Department of the Wellstar Hospital system provided evidence of the interconnection between brain function, mind, physical health, emotions, and finances.

Laura is endorsed by physicians, governments, celebrities, entrepreneurs, businesses, and individuals. She is acknowledged for her commitment to excellence in her work with clients and in the standard of training she provides in her state-authorized school of hypnosis, Professional Hypnosis Institute LLC.

Her many supporters, all treasured resources, include …

- Dr. Daniel Amen, the founder of Amen Clinics, best-selling author, medical expert, and pioneer in the field of brain health.

- The brilliant and talented Dr. Taz of Centre-Spring MD, a highly acclaimed integrative health physician in Atlanta who is regularly featured with Dr. Oz.

- Two of the most dedicated, kind, and patient-centered physicians, Dr. Patel and Dr. Dowdell, both outstanding sleep specialists and pulmonary physicians at Wellstar Hospital.

CHAPTER 4:

THAT GUN IN MY FACE
SET ME FREE

BY LAURA TEMIN

THE SETUP

By the time I got home, darkness had fallen. Little did I know, they were already there, in position, waiting. They knew who I was. They knew what I did. And they knew my routine. They were waiting for me.

Out of the corner of my eye, I saw one of the men slip under the closing garage door. The next thing I knew, he was looming over me, peering into my car window as I sat inside my parked car. And then suddenly, the handle of his gun smashed against my driver's seat window, sending a kaleidoscope of fragmented chunks of glass crashing in on me.

Frozen in time and space, I sat wide-eyed, dumbfounded, and trapped inside a closed garage, in a car that was turned off. It seemed that nothing but sheer terror stood between me and his gun.

But I was wrong. There was much more.

DANGER AND THE SURVIVAL RESPONSE

In the face of danger, your logical mind shuts down. Your thinking goes out the window. Instead, the most powerful part of you, your subconscious mind, comes to your rescue. That part of your mind steps in and takes over, automatically. That's how you were designed. Your subconscious mind is always there, ready to protect you.

Your primitive mind — the part of you that controls your breathing and swallowing and keeps your heart beating — comes equipped with a Survival Response. In the face of danger, the message is "run or fight." And if you can't do either, just freeze! The Survival Response is written into your DNA, and the program automatically operates when you can't. That's the power of your subconscious mind. It's your hero in times of need.

The Survival Response — fight, flight, or freeze — is just a temporary holding pattern until the immediate danger passes. Then, the thinking part of the brain comes forward again. Throughout every crisis, your subconscious mind continues coding and indexing every distressing detail of your experience and logging it into your memory bank so that it can warn you of similar impending danger in the future. Survival is all that matters.

What's reality?

The mind doesn't distinguish between a current danger, a past danger, and an anticipated danger as long as the imagined or remembered danger is vividly recalled in all its horrific detail. To your mind, a threat is a threat. Whether I actually have a gun in my face, or I replay the incident in my mind or anticipate being met with a gun in my face, my system will respond similarly.

A threat is a threat

A threat to survival can take many forms. For a child it can be a drunk parent or a bully at school. In business it can be a layoff or losing your best customer. It can be a divorce, a cancer diagnosis, or anything else that the mind perceives as threatening.

If you quit your job and invested your life savings into a cleaning franchise, and within a month a pandemic lockdown made it impossible for you to clean homes or offices, wouldn't that be a threat? If your spouse cheated on you in the past, and you come home early from work and they're out and you can't reach them by phone, your subconscious mind automatically associates this moment with the past, triggering old memories and sending fear chemicals throughout your system. This is how we're wired. The purpose is to protect you. But if we don't understand the survival instinct or how to use the mind, we can get stuck. Here's how it happens …

Four phases of crisis

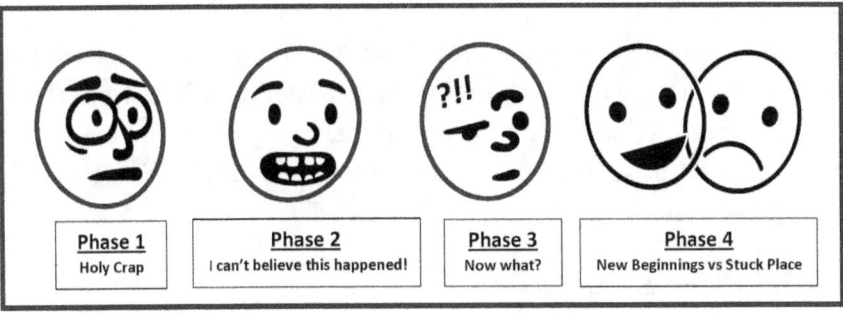

Phase 1: Holy crap — This is the moment when the mind finally comprehends what's happening. We're riddled with shock and fear. The Survival Response activates fight, flight, or freeze.

Phase 2: I can't believe this happened! — Grief, loss, anger, sadness, and lingering dismay follow as we process this event and our loss.

Phase 3: Now what? — We ponder and deal with the facts. We begin thinking about what to do: how to cope, manage, proceed, and so forth.

Phase 4: New beginnings versus stuck place — We start putting a plan together to move forward and pick up the pieces, maybe completely reinventing our life. Or we remain caught between the past and the future, frightened and hopeless, either living in yesterday or glorifying and mourning it. We're simply unable to find our way forward.

THE SUBCONSCIOUS MIND

Why do some people get stuck while others thrive? The answer ties back to the subconscious mind.

Remember, we're designed to be laser-focused on anything that threatens our survival. And the protective subconscious mind stores every detail that we've experienced. So, if I approach my garage and see something suspicious, my antenna goes up. I'm immediately pulled into yesterday, preparing for fight or flight.

Everyone experiences extreme situations. The single most deciding element separating those who thrive and master their lives from those who get stuck, is their relationship with their mind — the subconscious mind in particular, because our associations, expectations, and imagination live there.

Facts, feelings, and beliefs

Everything happens in the mind. The mind interprets every event and creates meaning. That meaning creates our beliefs. Our beliefs drive us and run our lives.

Here's an example. A mother and daughter came to see me. The daughter complained, "My mother worries about everything. It's driving me crazy." The mother looked down and said, "It's true. I can't help worrying." They determined that the worry began 5 years before. It turned out that the mother's best friend had discovered her own husband of 20 years had been leading a double life. The mother had known the couple for 15 years. Her friend's husband was a good man. The mother had spent lots of time with the couple, and she had never suspected he was "that kind of person." But he was.

Her mind told her that if she could be fooled by someone she had known for years, who else was fooling her? How could she trust her own judgment now? How could she trust anyone? Therefore, she concluded, the world wasn't safe, she wasn't safe, her daughter wasn't safe. That belief was an interpretation based on the events. The events were true. But was the interpretation really accurate? No. It was a generalization created by an interpretation — designed to protect her.

In the midst of a crisis, our emotions are more powerful than the logical part of the mind. We believe we're thinking logically, but actually we're driven by the underlying emotion and our past experiences. We see our interpretations as facts. We don't realize that we're stringing together a fact with a feeling with an interpretation and creating a belief.

ACCIDENTAL HYPNOSIS!

During an emotional upheaval, what we tell ourselves or what others say has more power in those moments than it ever could when we're feeling centered and grounded. That's because when we're overloaded, we're actually in a state of hypnosis. Accidental hypnosis. It doesn't mean that we are in a deep, dark trance, like in the movies, or that someone can extract our secrets without our control. It means that, when we have more on our plate than our resources can deal with, our emotions override our analytical abilities and we're more influenced by what we see, hear, and tell ourselves and the meaning we make of it. Brain research confirms this.[1]

That's why an interpretation made during a crisis has a lot of power. Unfortunately, most people don't know this. Beliefs that form in crisis moments become strongly held beliefs, and we carry them forward

---

1. "'Reality' is constructed by your brain. Here's what that means, and why it matters." By Brian Resnick, Jun 22, 2020, Vox Media (Online Article)

because we FEEL them. That's what happened to the mother. And that's typical for most of us.

The fleeting truth and the stuck place

The gun in my face created a belief that I was no longer safe in my home or in my business. That was true. But it was true only under specific conditions. The mind generalizes it into "I'm no longer safe," as if it's a universal truth.

When we're stuck, it's often because we are generalizing an experience with no distinctions. But those who thrive and master their minds learn to notice the distinctions. They refuse to get caught in the interpretations and stories they hear or tell themselves. What they do is reframe the story. They create a new, empowering interpretation and a vision to match.

In an interview with Elon Musk after he purchased Twitter, he spoke about this concept of survival — but applied it to business. He said that the news media intentionally focuses and sensationalizes the absolute worst things that happen in the world every day, because people are wired to pay attention to the tiger on their tail, not the delicious berries.[2] Survival is essential for businesses as well as individuals. News channels and social media businesses will lose eyes and ears and will die if they fail to catch our attention. Drama, trauma, and fear grab our attention. If you keep that in mind when you see horrific headlines, you won't be pulled in, and you'll have a better chance of feeling safe and grounded.

The story wins

What we hear and tell ourselves creates either a sense of hope or hopelessness. Fear or security. Not only within ourselves but within our families, our work, and the community. What we're told about our world, the economy, and one another impacts how we feel, think, and conduct our lives.

Accidental hypnosis is what happened to the mother when she learned that her best friend's husband wasn't who he seemed. Her interpretation created the belief that she wasn't safe. The stories she relives in

---

2. YouTube Video by Fox News, Apr 17, 2023 "Elon Musk reveals the goal of the new Twitter"

her mind feed her worry and keep it alive. The stuck person becomes a victim of their mind without their awareness.

The power of the mind — The great reframe

How do the Masters escape their demise? How do they come through bankruptcies to build empires? How do those who are diagnosed with cancer win the battle? And those who were abused? How do they survive and thrive?

Everything begins in the mind. We have much more power than we know, and when we face a crisis, the way we frame it in the mind either takes us forward or sets us back. Masters refuse to be bullied by their mind. They tell themselves they will find the way. Do they believe it? Sometimes. But other times, they just hold that thought until it takes root.

THE GIFT

The gun in my face forced me to make a choice. Do I live, or do I give up and die? I heard my voice rise up from inside of me, screaming, "NOOOOOOO!" I still don't know if I shouted that word or if it was the intensity of the decision to fight that screamed in my ear. And for one brief moment, his eyes met mine and I knew I was not alone. Something greater than me was working behind the scenes.

Somehow, I turned the motor on and clicked the garage door open. But not before the robber popped my trunk, grabbed my bag filled with $100,000 of gold and diamond jewelry (I worked in the jewelry business at the time), and sped off in the waiting car.

I was no longer safe in New York, and I knew that it was time to move. But I felt compelled to give the jewelry business one more try, because my partner and I had put everything we had into it and our business depended on both of us.

When a dream dies, another is born

My partner continued our business in New York while I moved to Georgia, attempting to open a new territory and escape the fear and danger that haunted me. Within a year, I was the target of another attack.

What I didn't tell you above was the reason I'd sat in my car with the motor turned off on that fateful day. I had attended a hypnosis conference that week and was captivated by what I had learned. I was listening to the hypnosis training on my car's CD player, thinking the CD was almost over.

What I also didn't mention was that after the gun-in-my-face robbery, I promised myself I would leave the business without guilt if it ever happened again.

HEARTFELT DESTINY LEADS THE WAY

That was 25 years ago.

I continued pursuing my interest in hypnosis in Georgia. There I met a hypnotherapist who dissolved the fear and anxiety that had resulted from the robberies. She became my mentor, and my new career path crystalized.

I returned to school for a graduate degree and a license in counseling psychology and marriage therapy. I continued building my skills in hypnotherapy and counseling and opened my practice. Today I'm the Clinical Director of Professional Hypnosis Institute Inc. — the only state-authorized school of hypnotherapy in the entire state of Georgia for over 23 years — where I help clients and teach hypnotherapy.

Mastery begins where our comfort level ends

We're creatures of habit. We may want things to change, but we don't want to change. We like things to be easy and comfortable.

To find your way in the darkness, let these steps guide you …

- Make the decision to survive and thrive
- Be curious and determined to find what's next
- Trust that you will
- Refuse to let other people's doubts or limitations interfere with your decision to move ahead
- Actively fill your mind with a bigger vision

- Focus on your wants, despite the doubts
- When doubts surface, learn how to build a bridge between your current beliefs and the ones you want
- Stop mentally rehearsing worst-case scenarios
- Find others who align with your vision
- Ask G-d or the Universe for guidance
- Look for evidence that something wonderful is waiting for you

Remember this

Each of us has a purpose, maybe many, and it changes over time. We're meant to keep moving forward. When one dream dies, another one is waiting to be born, *if we allow it*. There will always be challenges and crises to manage. We hate when they happen, but hindsight proves that they take us forward, make us stronger, and prepare us for the next milestone.

Behind the scenes, G-d and the forces in the Universe are laying the foundation for us and paving the way.

Refuse to believe the lies in your head. Learn how to use your subconscious mind to help you align with your goals. You may not know what they are, but I promise they will show themselves to you.

Pastor Joel Osteen's messages consistently encourage us to do our part, to keep getting back up, and to expect miracles. Here Joel Osteen and Laura Temin discuss beliefs.

Go online for more!

For more information regarding a free 15-minute phone consultation and to learn more about self-hypnosis, certification training, and Laura Temin's best-selling book, please visit the Anthology Author Resource page!

For more information regarding our authors,
please visit bestsellerpublishing.org/2023anthology!

About Albee Shanefelter

Albee Shanefelter lives in Silver Spring, Maryland, with his beautiful wife, Jenny, and two amazing children, Milo and Betty.

Previously, he was a Silicon Valley veteran, a key executive in building a $100 million business from scratch. This was sold to a Fortune 50 company — providing an 11x return to investors. He also managed strategic accounts for a technology start-up which was acquired for $6+ billion in the dot-com heyday.

Today, Albee is a Chronic Pain Warrior who has learned to live well around two intense chronic nerve pain conditions and now bone pain (metastatic bone cancer lesions). He is a thriving stage 4 cancer killer, documenting complementary methods to aid the ability of various cancer treatments to heal the body.

He is adjusting and adapting to become a highly competitive and WINNING champion in the budding adaptive golf community. Determined to use the journey as a force for good, Albee is now an author, speaker, and social entrepreneur launching his 3Bs organization.

For more information regarding our authors,
please visit bestsellerpublishing.org/2023anthology!

CHAPTER 5

3BS TO BE UNSTOPPABLE

BY ALBEE SHANEFELTER

When I was a global technology executive, the demands on my time outweighed my ability to take time off at will. My birthday was slammed with back-to-back-to-back calls, so I blocked the next morning off to get up and out to play a round of golf to celebrate. Afterward, as I was walking off the course, this strong burning sensation across my face emerged. Running to the clubhouse, thinking I had some kind of horrible chemicals on my hands that I'd rubbed on my face, I scrubbed and scrubbed, but it did nothing. I jetted to the car and headed back to the home office. On the way, the burning got worse and worse, so I rang my doctor and headed straight there.

I went in, and they thought it was shingles. If you've never had the pleasure of shingles or nerve pain, it is an intensely painful, electric, searing, shocking, special kind of pain. Shingles includes a big ugly rash, typically across the midsection of your body. The doctor gave me some medicine and told me to come back in a week.

During the week, the pain grew more intense, and an ice-pick-to-the-temple sensation emerged. At the follow-up, they were all huddling in the corner. They made me sit down, and then said they were "very sorry" but I had trigeminal neuralgia (TN). Me: "Okay, so what do we do now?" They gave me more new medicines to try and sent me on my way.

When I returned to my home office, I searched "What is TN?" online. Good Lord, to my shocking horror I read about this lifelong, extremely painful, incurable condition known as the Suicide Disease. I did not process getting this news very well and had an absolute traumatic meltdown.

Being a scrappy fellow, I went at this very hard, with all the medicines and procedures, including multiple brain surgeries. The last one was partially botched. When I woke up in the recovery room, I knew something was very, very, very wrong. The ice pick sensation had faded, but now my teeth killed, the right side of my face was swollen as if from a massive punch, my face was completely numb — yet somehow my cheek, gums, and tongue burned unbelievably intensely. "How could this be possible? I'm on a morphine drip!"

Surgeons thought for sure it would settle and then pass, yet week after week, it did not. We had damaged the nerve, and I was left with a secondary condition called anesthesia dolorosa (AD).

During this time, the looping storms between my ears were loud and exhausting, in addition to the pain itself and the side effects of all the medicines. "Why me? How am I going to survive this?" On and on I went, so I joined a few online TN support groups and befriended a few other TN patients.

One morning, I logged in and tried to find one of my fave TN buddies, who had such a great attitude, only to find out he was gone — like *gone* gone. Dead. NOOOOOOO! We were just chatting last night! Whether it was an overdose or an accidental toxic cocktail, we will never know.

Turns out this is not uncommon in this chronic nerve-pain community. Nerve pain is a special sort of ugliness. All I could think was that there had to be a better way to help all these people, and that's when I knew I'd have to do something to help others find a light in the darkness.

My mantra had been BeStrong, BeWell, and BeKind. I started to share this with others, and sure enough, it had an immediate, positive impact on their lives.

BUILDING YOUR RESILIENCE

It's human nature to run from pain, yet pain is unavoidable in our lives and in our businesses. YOU are NOT powerless. You are the captain of your own ship, the author of your own book, the creator of your own next chapter. You, too, can find meaning and acceptance in the most horrible of events that happen in your life and redirect it all toward forward positive progress.

Pain is unavoidable in life, but the suffering is optional.

— Buddha? The Dalai Lama?
(The debate over the original citation continues ...)

Let me introduce you to the 3Bs and their meanings.

BeStrong

Being physically strong is great, especially when you are miserable and life keeps punching you. It is an amazing sensation to be strong when you don't feel well — I highly recommend it. Yet there is much more beyond physical strength: learning to pause and process events and then taking intentional action, as opposed to leaping from one knee-jerk reaction to another. Being strong is being honest with yourself and others about your true reality. Being strong is being open to the neuroscience of your own brain's plasticity and embracing a growth mindset and a resilient warrior mentality.

For EVERY successful team I've built and managed, in 100% of them the key was simply finding what was important to people in their real lives and then enabling them to achieve those things while delivering their results to the organization. You need to look inside yourself, identify and learn what motivates and inspires you, and then use those motivators intentionally, daily. Save willpower for only the times when you actually need it, because once you rely upon willpower and adrenaline to get you through every rough moment, your probability of success falls off a cliff. It is not sustainable.

Last, being strong means being strong enough to say, "Hey, I need to take a break," and NOT just continue to grind past the point of your effectiveness. In the short term, you are producing low-quality output that will cost more time to fix later, but even worse, you are spending some of tomorrow's energy today. In the long term, there are even more drastic effects on the organization. The point here is, you do have control. You can move from feeling powerless to being powerful — you can BeStrong!

BeWell

Being well is making micro-improvements toward improving your health regardless of the s*** show that is happening in your life, your business, and the world. Being well is knowing your Magic Number, which is how many hours of sleep you need to function at a high level, and routinely achieving it. Being well is scheduling SmartBreaks into your daily schedule that encompass the 3Bs, such as a guided meditation with noise-canceling headphones, a walk, yoga, or stretching. Being well is becoming aware of what you are putting into your body and slowly migrating toward healthier inputs. Being well is adopting solid, full-body exercise routines.

Being well is understanding, documenting, and staying on point with your priorities. Being well is spending time with your loved ones regardless of how busy you may be. Being well is spending time with plants and animals, which accelerates your ability to recharge and recover. To level up, you can learn to garden, to farm or urban farm, or to take care of a few house plants, which *ahem* is my level today. Being well is staying hydrated. Being well is understanding all the effects of medicines and stimulants — java or others — in your daily routine.

BeKind

Being kind is both inward and outward. The old adage "You cannot give to others what you do not have yourself" is timeless. This inward work may be the hardest work you ever do in your life, but it will serve you extremely well, forever. Mirror work is GOLD, so head over to the mirror to see if you can even smile at your reflection for a few seconds. At first, I could not smile at that person at all, so do not fret. Start there, then work up to 5 seconds, then to 15 seconds, and onwards. The end goal is one full minute. You can get there.

Being kind is being worthy of accepting joy, love, happiness, and abundance. Go back to the mirror and tell that reflection that you are worthy. How'd that go? Well, I'm not sure about you, but the person doing the talking to me was not only unkind but often downright cruel. What the heck? So do not fret; just keep practicing. Being kind is learning to recognize and interrupt negative self-talk, then mindfully replacing it with positive, productive thoughts that you do want to have — the beauty is, you do not even have to believe. You just have to do it. This is truly magical.

Once you make headway, you can start to apply this outward to your employees, suppliers, partners, and customers. "Kill 'em with kindness" and "Be hard on the issue, soft on the person" are the best pieces of advice anyone could give. As you work through your day, observe your initial thoughts — how you would typically respond and react — then change them mindfully to respond in a positive, productive, and collaborative manner.

The blame game, cover-your-a**, and us-versus-them mentalities that run rampant across all organizations are far from productive. Do they enable you to achieve your stated desired outcomes? Sure, we want to document lessons learned, fix broken processes, institute better early-warning systems, and prevent issues from reoccurring, but focusing on forward progress toward your goals and objectives will serve you best, time after time.

A Helping Hand

Through the years I compiled notes on how I used the 3Bs to live again and live well around the TN and the AD. After a few venture successes and failures, I decided to compile these into a book: *The Battle-Proven Path to Living Better TODAY* was born.

A decade after that first TN diagnosis, I felt sicker and sicker but was still living well. All my doctors and all the service providers just kept saying, "Oh, it's related to the TN."

Unfortunately, not so — it was prostate cancer, thriving and spreading wildly throughout my body. Getting the news of aggressive, terminal stage 4 cancer is traumatic. Yet here I am, becoming an author and a speaker — the 3Bs have enabled more than 100 others and their families to learn to live well around lifelong, incurable, unpleasant conditions.

Trying to make sense of this late-stage cancer, I received this message from above. It was time to drink my own Kool-Aid. The first book was pretty good, but the Universe and God were saying, "You did well, but how about we make this much better!"

Finding meaning in the cancer diagnosis enabled me to fast-track down the path to acceptance and made the book so much better. Then I received a second message from God and the Universe: "You need to take the 3Bs message further and reach the millions of others who are left to suffer!" 3Bs (.org) was born.

Seeing others embrace the mantra of living the 3Bs and mastering their own awareness and action has been amazingly gratifying. The gratitude and love from them and their families has powered me through cancer treatments, TN flares, and daily AD challenges to the point where I am already accomplishing things that the doctors said would not be possible. BAM!

If you or a loved one has a chronic condition or just needs a helping hand to move forward, 3Bs (.org) is here to help light a path — the battle-proven path — in the darkness for them.

Illuminating the path for souls throughout the world

As it turns out, the issues are the same both in life, with its chronic, unpleasant conditions, and in business, through its ups and downs and ins and outs. Embracing the mantra of BeStrong, BeWell, and BeKind has already turned around the lives of so many folks to put them on a battle-proven path to a better life.

You, too, can join us to positively impact the lives of millions of others around the globe. Just remember: tiny micro-improvements via the 3Bs lead to unimaginable leaps forward.

- Hire us to come speak to your leadership team and entire organization.
- Purchase one of the 3Bs online class offerings for someone you love.

- After I officially publish my book, acquire copies of *Be Strong. Be Well. Be Kind.* for your organization. Visit the Anthology Author Resource page for more information.

- Listen to the *3BNation* podcast and engage with the 3Bs community on social media.

I would not have picked this path by choice; alas, here we are … so be it. Let's use it as a FORCE for GOOD in this world and see how many souls we can illuminate.

Be Strong, Be Kind, Be Well,
Albee, Founder of the 3Bs

About Selina Delangre

 Selina Delangre is the best-selling author of *In Her Element: Sea Salt, Surrender, and the Journey to a Whole Life* and the owner of the most loved sea salt brand in the world, Celtic Sea Salt®. For over 30 years, she has led the sea salt industry through trends and innovation and received endless testimonials from customers who have incredibly great results using her sea salts and products. She sources sea salts from locations all over the world, including France, Spain, Portugal, Mexico, Guatemala, and Hawaii. Her passion to provide the world with clean, high-mineral salt has grown her brand into the most trusted sea salt available.

Selina is also the mother of three, the oldest of whom was born with cerebral palsy. Selina's journey of seeking out healing solutions came from her need to help repair her son's brain damage. She ultimately began questioning the cause and effect of our actions and intentions and, in turn, began to study lifestyle choices that promote optimal well-being.

For more information regarding our authors,
please visit bestsellerpublishing.org/2023anthology!

CHAPTER 6:

RESILIENCE THROUGH SURRENDER

BY SELINA DELANGRE

Stepping into the role as a business owner wasn't something I thought I would ever do. Looking back on myself as a child or young adult, I realize every experience we have in life is a preparation for what we are called to do and be.

I am a believer that our souls agree to come into this life and have the experiences to empower our expansions so we can contribute more to the whole experience and expansions of life. This could be as a mother, father, sister, brother, employee, business owner — whatever identity we possess is a divine agreement and plan our soul makes before we are born. I am an uplifter. My personal mission statement is "I am a reflection of anyone who comes into my life, of their fullest potential."

What I have recognized is, we all have our own worries and insecurities that come from a sort of imposter syndrome. We use our challenges as either an excuse to give up and not expand or an opportunity to be a better person.

We also can use our challenges as an excuse to escape, with whatever means give us that sense of relief from the pain or stresses of life. I have had my share of escapes that I am not ashamed of but also not proud of.

My most recent example is the freedom of using weed as an escape. I used the justification of its capabilities of increasing my appetite when I didn't feel hungry because I was stressed, or the way it could shift my mind from stressful emotions. At the end of the day, how did I feel after the escape was over? I realized the feeling was not one of victory but of disappointment. I was unable to tap into a source that could give me the feeling not only of relief but also of victory that I could find a place of peace and a solution without the weed.

STRENGTH IN CLARITY

We all struggle with the fear of uncertainty. But it is a fear that doesn't serve us, and we take the path of familiarity, which produces the same reality. I have belief now that this fear of uncertainty can be shifted to an enthusiastic response to the unknown, with faith that it will always work out to be just as it should be. And sometimes this is not what I thought I wanted, but it's exactly what I needed.

I find that when I am in an experience and observe others in life and compare my life to theirs, I feel as though I am an imposter. I feel like they have their act together and I am struggling with my own insecurities. This makes me feel unworthy of what I have achieved. In today's age, with all the social media influences, I think this is becoming even more prevalent in society. These platforms were intended to keep people updated but are becoming more addictive and associated with our self-worth.

I am growing into the wisdom to compare myself only to yesterday's version of me and to see how I can do and be better. This releases me from the negative emotion that comes with envy or jealousy, and it releases a positive emotion of joy for the gratitude that I have another day to make a change in myself. I have also removed myself from social media exposure to support this practice of self-worth.

I love this quote from Eckhart Tolle: "All negativity is caused by an accumulation of psychological time and denial of the present. Unease, anxiety, tension, stress, worry — all forms of fear — are caused by too much future, and not enough presence. Guilt, regret, resentment, grievances, sadness, bitterness, and all forms of non forgiveness are caused by too much past, and not enough presence."

When I wrote my book *In Her Element*, I accomplished a lot of self-forgiveness — which is something I recommend for self-expansion. I also recommend writing a book, whether you go to print and publish it or not. It is the best exercise to look at yourself and gain clarity on what life is about.

Through the reflection of remembering your stories in life, you realize you made it through, whatever it was. You did it. When you realize you did it, you also gain confidence that you can do it again. The other day I was reunited with Ali, a counselor coach I used to go to. He said to me, "Selina, I see you, and you need to look at yourself in the mirror and say 'I see you' to the you that you have become."

When I am approached by someone who has read my book and they say they have so much more admiration and respect for me, I want to reflect that back to them — knowing if we all wrote a book about ourselves and our stories, we would have a different experience from others. There are so many opportunities for us to judge others, but if we knew more about them, I am sure our opinion would not be the same.

My mom is 86 years old, and I hear her saying frequently, "I didn't do anything special in life." I think about how many people look at their life and have these thoughts. I tell her, "Are you kidding? You brought five children into this world, and they all have made an impact on something in their lives. You were a role model of integrity and grit. That's something to be proud of."

I watch my daughter Carla do so much for so many people, putting her own needs and expansions on the sideline. If she would write a book about herself, the way she helped me write mine, she would have the same admiration coming to her. Her constant reminder, "You are exactly where you should be in this time and space," is my reminder to be in the moment.

If we could look at ourselves the way others see us, we would love ourselves so much more. We are our worst critics, and we need to stop this. We need to tap into a reflection of how the universe and God the creator see us and know that it wasn't by chance we came in the bodies we have and the families we have.

Being clear is a way of co-creating with God the life you want instead of a life you will regret.

For me, finding my way through life without substances is a victory. It gives me the opportunity to tap into a power and force that is unlimited. I have been able to achieve this through the practice of meditation. I thought I was experiencing the power of meditation until I went to a weeklong retreat that gave me the opportunity to authentically feel what it truly means to become a new you. I went to the Joe Dispenza one. But today there are so many options of exploring meditation; just choose one and make it your discipline to become a better version of yourself.

I appreciated the practice doing a walking meditation. This taught me how to bring that train of thought into my everyday life. When the temptation of relapsing into the reaction mode versus the response mode occurs, I can bring myself back to the new person I have become and not return to my old habits of stress and worry, which produce results I don't want in my life anymore.

We are all so busy, and it's okay to be busy. This is what we came here to do in these physical bodies. It's so much more satisfying to be busy with peace of mind and joy. We are all giving so much of ourselves to others. I am learning to give some of that love to myself. If we give more to ourselves in the present, we have more to give to others in the future.

SURRENDER

I was 20 years old when I had my first child. I was so confident I would give birth to a thriving, healthy baby. But I was gifted with a son who was born with cerebral palsy and epilepsy. Little did I know, this experience was to shape me into who I am today. Even though my son Dominic never spoke a word in the 28 years he was alive, he taught me more about being a person with compassion and empathy than anyone I have ever met.

He taught me that there was no option to give up. According to Oxford Languages, resilience is "the capacity to withstand or to recover quickly from difficulties." This equipped me to be the CEO of a 45-year-old company that owns the most recognized brand of sea salt in the world, Celtic Sea Salt.

Imagine being faced with the daily needs of a child, but you have absolutely no experience with those needs and no internet to search the "how-tos" that we have at our fingertips today. Your next best option is tapping into the supernatural resource that comes from God, our source of power. And to do this and maintain happiness comes from the ability to surrender and trust that each day will offer solutions.

I built this company with the intention to provide for my son and my two daughters. I built it to offer a livelihood for all the employees I had over the years. And I did this with as much integrity and gratitude as life would allow me.

I extended this intention to provide for my employees and my customers. I learned so much from reading books and listening to tapes on how to better yourself every day. I learned that the real competition was to be better than I was the day before. I feel most resilience comes from the desire to be better and do better, no matter what life has to offer. There are leaders who influence us to make more money and grow our company. But at the end of the day, my force came from spiritual leaders.

Apart from the Eckhart Tolle's words I quoted earlier in this chapter, I found myself influenced greatly by shared wisdom such as …

- **Wayne Dyer:** "You cannot always control what goes on outside. But you can always control what goes on inside."
- **Joe Dispenza:** "A memory without the emotional charge is called wisdom," and "To be empowered — to be free, to be unlimited, to be creative, to be genius, to be divine — that is who you are …"
- **Deepak Chopra:** "Every person is a God in embryo. Its only desire is to be born."

These are some of the words that I would put up in my home or office for my attention as much as possible, to remind myself that I am not alone and that there are people whose words can help me to see experiences in a different way. I wake up every morning and pray to see the world through God's eyes. And I pray to reflect God's power and the unlimited resources from the universe.

So, it is in the power of surrender that I find resilience, like the teacher Michael Singer shares in his book *The Surrender Experiment*. I'm not talking about "surrender" as described in the dictionary ("ceasing resistance to an enemy or opponent and submit to their authority"). I mean the surrender in trusting that God will always be there for you, and you just need to get out of the way.

I encourage you to find a method of meditation that will connect you to your higher self. This has proved to be the best form of resilience for me. In closing, the unknown is always a source of stress and anxiety. Trust and faith in knowing it is all as it should be lessens the effects of stress and anxiety.

I surrendered.

And the future remains what it is and what it needs to be.

For more information regarding our authors,
please visit bestsellerpublishing.org/2023anthology!

About Jess Hughes

Jess Hughes, CEO of Jess Hughes Media and Illuminated Press™, is an audience growth expert, international speaker, three-time #1 international best-selling author, TV host of *The Creative LifeShow*™, and visionary who created *The Creative Lifebook*™ series.

Her passion is to support hidden-gem entrepreneurs in amplifying their voice, stepping into the spotlight, leading with confidence, and making a true impact in the world through educational programs, courses, and coaching.

She guides members through her three-phase signature solution to IGNITE their potential within her Creative LifeTribe of Conscious Creatives, helps them LEAP into action by inviting them to contribute to *The Creative Lifebook* series, and empowers them to MAXIMIZE their impact in her business growth accelerator, Illuminate.

Her resilience training is rooted in single-parenting seven children after overcoming addiction and identity loss. This has given her a powerful voice that deeply resonates with a wide range of audiences.

She has been featured on ABC, NBC, FOX, and TED, and in *Forbes*, Chopra, and more.

For more information regarding our authors,
please visit bestsellerpublishing.org/2023anthology!

CHAPTER 7:

BACK TO THE WILD
(RECLAIMING AND REIGNITING AT ROCK BOTTOM)

BY JESS HUGHES

Life has an extraordinary way of coming full circle, as long as we persevere and refuse to give up, even when faced with the darkest of moments.

As a child, I was a wild, imaginative spirit, brimming with passion for dancing, exploring forests, and collecting unicorns — unwavering in my conviction that I would be the one to uncover the existence of these mythical creatures. The memories of uninhibited freedom — as I spun and twirled to my dad's '60s Motown tunes or energetically danced to Van Halen's "Jump" and Michael Jackson's "Thriller" in the '80s — still resonate within me.

My boundless passion for creativity thrived. But somewhere along the journey from childhood to adulthood, I lost my willingness to be seen. As I faced the limitations imposed by society and sought the approval of others, my creativity was stifled. I became painfully shy and transformed into a wallflower at every dance.

My creative gifts were eclipsed by a world that placed logic and analysis on a pedestal. Doubt infiltrated my spirit, and I began to question everything about myself.

Throughout my journey, I found myself oscillating between crippling self-doubt and extraordinary moments of stepping into my genius zone — only to self-sabotage before experiencing sustainable success. I went from being an all-American athlete — at a Division 1, Big Ten school for rowing with a straight path to the Olympics — to experiencing the debilitating effects of depression, loneliness, and feeling misunderstood. My visionary dreams of creating a tremendous impact as a creative entrepreneur were constantly undermined by my lack of self-belief and support.

Despite my efforts to create successful businesses, I found myself repeating the same pattern of self-sabotage and burning out. The vicious cycle left me feeling powerless and defeated.

Feeling misunderstood and lost, I eventually dropped out of college to take a year off to recover. During that time, I found the courage to start a successful business that offered a glimmer of hope and purpose. But, despite my achievements, I never returned to college. Instead, I pursued my entrepreneurial ventures with all my might, driven by a deep-seated passion to prove to myself and others that I was capable of creating an impact and living a life of purpose.

Then I found myself pregnant with twins, and single. And life detoured again …

GREATNESS AND LIMITATIONS

In the years that followed, I married and had five more children — all while pushing forward through the ups and downs of starting two more businesses that earned six figures. However, I continued to face setbacks and challenges along the way.

As a passionate artist, I possess an incredible depth of emotional experience, which was both a gift and a curse. I found myself swinging between moments of being called to greatness and the limitations of everyday reality. Raising seven remarkable children and managing the demands of a household of nine added to the challenge.

Those years were filled with immense joy, but also some of the loneliest times as I felt like a complete outlier from other mothers. I wasn't a full-time mom, and I struggled to spread my wings sustainably in business. A deep rift in my marriage occurred only a few years into it, yet I stayed silent and endured for the sake of my children. I now realize that retreating into my mind during those times was dangerous, and I needed to find a way to break free from the limitations that were holding me back.

I lost my identity, my confidence, and my voice. I felt like a failure and wanted to hide from the world. It wasn't until I lost my father to cancer that I began my descent to the rock bottom that would finally be the catalyst for change.

RECLAIM AND REIGNITE

Have you ever been trapped on a relentless roller coaster of emotions, feeling like you're battling between different worlds? I know that struggle all too well. I was shackled by anxiety, living a life where everything appeared flawless on the outside — a picture-perfect family with beautiful children and an exquisite home. But behind closed doors, the facade crumbled and the inner turmoil persisted. The struggle was real, and I found myself withdrawing from everyone around me, feeling trapped in my own mind.

Was it even in the realm of possibility to find the courage to speak up? To change everything? To leave what was no longer serving me and create the life that lit me from within?

Rock bottom is an excellent teacher.

How often do we let the fear of failure and the comfort of smallness hold us back? How often do we sacrifice our own needs and desires to please others? How long will we wait before we realize that living in pain is not living at all? I used to believe that isolating myself from the world would protect others from my struggles, but in doing so, I lost the essence of who I truly was.

The solution became apparent: I had to reclaim my voice and purpose, reigniting the ember of self-belief within me. I had to fully embrace my unique energetic signature and step boldly into the light, shining brightly for all to see. I needed to let my soul's purpose guide me, opening my heart and banishing fear from the driver's seat, allowing my heart to lead the way.

I was being called forward to do great things.

How could I possibly know that things bigger than my wildest dreams were waiting for me on the other side of leaping into the unknown? Somehow, I needed to find the fuel to ignite that belief within. I had to become willing to change.

In January 2018, I landed in rehab for substance addiction, and a few months later I spent time in an eating disorder treatment center.

It was when the only way to proceed forward was to walk directly through the pain that I became willing to look at the truth of my life.

Pain has a way of focusing our attention. I became willing to change. My life had come to a screeching halt, and the house of cards had collapsed around me. My old ways of numbing out to avoid the pain of a complete disconnection with my soul were out of the closet and now in the light.

I had a choice to make …

Was I going to go back to life as I knew it, or could I somehow find my voice and advocate for the vision I had for my soul and purpose?

Despite great fear, I found the courage to change everything. It was as if the universe had been bringing me to my knees (on repeat) so I would finally stop going it alone in my life.

I found my voice. I left my marriage. I began life again, this time clean and sober. Even as a single mom of seven kids, my heart was on fire to never play small, ever again.

What if things bigger than our wildest dreams are waiting for us on the other side of leaping into the unknown? How can we find the fuel to ignite that belief within ourselves? Are we willing to change to make it happen?

We all have a creative genius inside, clamoring to lead. To be seen, to be heard, to step into the spotlight and be fully expressed.

To step into visibility, as our authentic selves.

It wasn't until I became willing to step into the light and seek help that I discovered that adversity can be our greatest teacher and resiliency our greatest asset. When all the cards are stacked against you, like they were for me, it can be easy to give up.

Do you know the stats for female entrepreneurs? Only 4.2% ever make an annual revenue of seven figures a year; 88% of them never cross six figures.[3]

When I finally found my voice, answered my calling to start my creative business, and embraced visibility as the fastest way to connect with an audience, it was like I had strapped myself to a rocket ship.

Though I started my business in September 2020, intending to become a full-time painter, the engineer and visionary in me quickly saw the opportunity in front of me in the online space. Thanks to the COVID-19 shutdown, I went online, like many, to find connection and opportunity. And my highest calling as a creative thought leader and expert in my space was to be found.

I realized that people buy the artist, not the art. If I became highly visible, my chances for success would increase. People must move through the know-like-trust process to buy.

I went from $0 in income, with $0 in start-up cash, to crossing six figures in only eight months. I joined entrepreneur groups and began to share my story, overcoming addiction and pursuing my dream of entre-preneurship despite parenting seven children on my own.

I was asked to guest on podcasts, which led to being asked to share my story in my first book. I became an international best-selling author. This lit the fire of momentum and opened doors to interviews on regional and national TV and eventually to a feature in *Forbes* magazine — just eight months after starting my company. In doing so, I realized that visibility is the number one foundation for sales, and that stepping into leadership to fearlessly share my authentic self is what enabled others to resonate with and connect to different facets of my story.

Connection to others IS the most powerful thing on earth.

I began to forge that connection within, solidify my purpose here on earth, and step into the boldness of sharing my voice and perspec-tive with others. We can change from focusing on our limitations to becoming limitless, stepping into imperfect action to learn via big experiences that expand us, and then using strategy to maximize and

---

3. Women Entrepreneurs Statistics, written by Jenifer Kuadli for LegalJobs Blog, Last Accessed May 20, 2023

leverage the growth and visibility of doing big things — like writing, public speaking, coaching, and mentoring others. I realized that when we ignite this belief, the sky isn't even the limit to what is possible.

Only two and a half years later, I'm on track to cross seven figures in my business as a digital CEO and visionary. I'm leading other creatives to step into their genius zone and embrace full visibility to become well known and highly paid. Collectively, in doing so, we can reteach the world how to think about art and creativity.

I have returned to being that wild, vibrant, sparkly, creative leader. I am a thought leader. I have now worked with thousands of creatives to ignite their vision and create collaborative experiences for them to leap big. I help them see how to maximize those results to grow an audience that is obsessed with them.

I teach hidden-gem entrepreneurs how to amplify their voices to become well known and highly paid in a way that works for them, so that collectively we can illuminate the world.

In the end, I'm an engineer of the creative mind who has found a solution to rapidly grow captivated audiences who are deeply connected and committed. And it is through the adversity and challenges that I have developed the expert-level resilience to step fully into my genius zone.

And that fiery little girl obsessed with art and unicorns?

My membership for conscious creatives, The Creative LifeTribe, has nicknamed me "Chief Unicorn Sparkles."

How's that for a return to ultimate freedom of expression?

Let's glitter it up!

To learn more about how I can pour gasoline on your visibility so you can step fully into your authentic voice and grow an audience that is obsessed with you, come join in and play in my playground at my website for Jess Hughes Media.

To read the #1 international best-selling book series that I brought from thin air into reality as a collaborative amplification of 175 creative voices, thought leaders, wellness experts, artists, and creatives, you can purchase these at the website for *The Creative Lifebook.*

For links and further information, please visit the Anthology Author Resource page.

About Rami Donahoe, MS

Best-selling author Rami Donahoe, MS, has two decades of experience working as a crisis counselor, a child protective agent, and a dynamic K–12 school counselor in both Hawaii and California. The author is known for her motivational content that pushes people to reach their full potential. She has been called through Christ Jesus and therefore does not produce this work alone. Rami's two favorite Bible verses are Proverbs 3:5 and 1 Corinthians 10:13, which focus on trust and faith in God.

Rami is a strong advocate for Christ-centered education and alternative learning environments. She has a passion for sharing these educational options with families to give their children their best chance for success in school, college, and their careers.

Rami has previously published *Christian Focus in a Blurry World* and is an established Christian music artist. She is also the best-selling author of *Fight Flex Flight™: A Faith-Based Strategy Guide for Parents Concerned About Their Child and Public School.*

Find out about her success in coaching and consulting, free resources, and music at the website for Rami Positive Space.

For more information regarding our authors,
please visit bestsellerpublishing.org/2023anthology!

CHAPTER 8:

THREE MINDSETS FOR RESILIENCE
(PROVERBS 3:5, 1 CORINTHIANS 10:13, AND ABC)

BY RAMI DONAHOE, MS

I have had plenty of down moments in my life, but I'm just going to share one. I'll take you to a place in time where I involuntarily ended up wearing an orange vest, an orange hat, and work gloves, and getting searched twice a day. I ended up in the Orange County California Work Service Program in my sophomore year of high school. That is not where I thought I was going to be.

Our supervisor was called Mr. John, and he would grade us on each work day. Mr. John would drive us to our Saturday eight-hour mandatory work session, search our hearty crew for contraband, and make sure we were all putting 100% into every job we were doing for restitution community service hours. At that point in my life I was pretty used to getting negative consequences for my ignorant choices. I would get in-school suspensions, off campus suspensions, and Saturday School detentions. But this was different. This time I could not simply zone out or complete simple mindless worksheets to get credit for my consequential time.

In this case, as Mr. John yelled at us to "Get into it!" I realized that something in my life's journey had gone very wrong. Our job was to clear out hundreds of slippery ice plants in a beach community. As I stood wearing this orange hat and orange vest and getting searched twice every Saturday with Mr. John's added flair for yelling out orders, I started to wonder if this was really happening to me. There I stood, trying to complete my community service hours, looking like a neon pumpkin as all these people in board shorts and bikinis with their surfboards and umbrellas strolled by on their way to a day of fun and sun at the beach. This was my reality. This was my consequence for choosing to break the law. That realization did not feel comfortable.

As I was trying to pull the ice plants out with my tools, while avoiding the hundreds of snails on the ground and on the plants, Mr. John barked, "Lean into it, Rami! Get down into it!"

"Mr. John, if I do … the snails are gonna get squashed all over my best jeans."

"I don't care. You're here to work for us because of the choices that you made. Come on, get down into it or else I'm going to grade you a D for the day!"

Yes, you are right, Mr. John, I thought. *This is my consequence.* I was assigned to 25 days of work. If you received three As in a row for good work, they would subtract one of your days. I decided I was going to get down into it. I bent down into it as my knees felt the squish of every squash as the shells cracked into my jeans … *my favorite jeans.* I thought, *Well, how did I end up here?* The way that I ended up there was indulging in angry feelings and making bad choices to express my anger.

I met a lot of kids during those service hours. We would speak very quickly either while we were working or when we were on our lunch break. The number one question we all had was: "How did you get in here?" We would exchange stories of our past indiscretions. I had to embellish my stories because they weren't as cool as the others'. Let's face it, vandalism and petty theft are not really that exciting compared to assault, grand theft auto, and high-level felonies. But that's where it hit me that what I did was really, really wrong. These were serious, hardened kids with heavy crimes. I was supposed to be a Christian kid. How did I get there?

I was in trouble with the law, ditching school and getting the lowest grades I could. My reality finally caught up with me: *I'm stuck working for free, in the hot sun*, I thought. *No one trusts me, and my grades are telling everyone I am a complete idiot.* I finally realized it was time to turn things around. God blessed me with a full-time compassionate probation officer, whom I loved. He was a great motivator and was hoping I would find a reason to change.

THREE MINDSETS FOR RESILIENCE

The Proverbs 3:5 mindset

> *Trust in the Lord with all your heart and lean not on your own understanding. In all your ways acknowledge him, and he will make your path straight.*

God will make your path straight. He will. If you just trust in Him, acknowledge Him, and say, "Jesus, I know You got me; hallelujah." If you choose not to trust in Him, you will not see the miracles or feel the freedom of letting your cares be taken care of by God. We lose in life when we lean on what we see and think we know, while we should trade what we think we know for trusting in God in the supernatural. (2 Corinthians 5:7)

Trusting in the Lord is scary. Is there really an entity out there who cares about me, no matter what? What will happen if I stop worrying — will I forget to solve the problem? No. We know that in the Bible it states worrying will not add a single hour to your life (Luke 12:25–31). Pastor Steven Furtick said something very valuable in one of his many brilliant sermons: "I" is at the center of anxiety.

He continued to express that we need to exchange our "I" for His eye, which is always on us ("When Anxiety Attacks").[4] We can't do everything on our own, and we are not designed to do everything on our own. That's why God created a mate for Adam at the beginning of creation.

There is harmony in working with God and seeing who He places in our lives to overcome anxiety, worry, and weary times. Start with a prayer

---

4. YouTube Video by Elevation Church, October 17, 2016, "When Anxiety Attacks"

to release your worry to the Lord. Surrender anything that is preventing you from having peace in your life, such as anger and unforgiveness.

Breathe out the anxiety, and give yourself permission to submit these things to God. Tell God you love Him and repeat the words "He will make my path straight." I have found absolute peace in surrendering my fears, cares, and worries to Him. Right now, I agree in prayer with you that you will experience the same peace.

The Corinthians 10:13 mindset

> *No temptation has overtaken you except what is common to mankind. And God is faithful; he will not let you be tempted beyond what you can bear. But when you are tempted, he will also provide a way out so that you can endure it.*

I have said this verse in my head numerous times when I was tempted, especially when I was tempted to go back to my old lifestyle or when I was dating.

On one occasion, I was really tempted to hang out over at a young gentleman's apartment late into the night. I knew it was wrong. I knew I had no business going to some boy's apartment where I would be tempted to have sex. I could not say no. I just sat in this boy's car, looking at the entryway to my home. *If I could just get out and leave this car!* I could not move because, inside, I really wanted to go to his apartment and extend the evening.

Well, I was not going to find strength in myself, so I decided to turn to 1 Corinthians 10:13, a verse that came to mind: "No temptation has seized you." I thought to myself, *And God, you're going to provide a way of escape for me.* I just breathed a heavy breath.

The young gentleman said, "You don't want to come to my house, do you?"

There it is! My escape! I said, "No." He was okay and there was no problem, almost like a supernatural mind trick had happened or something. He dropped me off at home.

We spoke later and this boy said, "I don't know what happened to me. I never would have done that. Why did I let you go? I don't even know!"

I let him know: "I prayed. That's what happened, and I thank you for letting me off the hook." Pray through it. God will just give you that peace that passes all understanding (Philippians 4:6–7).

I can fail by myself, but I can win with Christ.

ABC

To address my former destructive behavior, I adopted a new phrase, "Always Be Creating." Instead of destroying, I'm going to be creating. A lot of us have a tremendous amount of nervous energy inside of us. This usually means we need to be doing or creating something to release it. We could binge on Netflix or Disney+, which I've done plenty of times. However, we will not get our energy out that way. We need to start creating things that are beautiful and meaningful.

I've had students who expressed a huge interest in destroying things and wanted a military career with a focus on demolition. While I was happy that these students were exploring careers for their future, they did not see the full picture. I asked the Army recruiters to come and talk to these students about the actual job description for a Special Forces Engineer (SFE).

To the students' surprise, it turns out there is a significant amount of creating and construction involved in being an SFE. The recruiters informed the students that they would also have to clean up what they destroyed. Many kids with anger and anxiety issues have tons of energy, but they need direction as to where that energy should be properly allocated.

Always Be Creating — get your kids to write stories or poetry, compose music, draw, build, or invent something that solves a problem. During my times of turmoil, I exchanged my boredom and idleness for creating and performing music. This helped channel my energy in a positive manner.

MAKING BIG CHANGES

I finally made the decision to change my life of destruction to one of a godly person. What was my final trigger? My wonderful Christian mother used to ask me, "Why can't you just be good?" And I said, "I'd be pretending."

My mother replied, "Just pretend, and see how it feels."

I decided *I should try this.* I tried "being good." And while I did not earn enough As to decrease the duration of my community service, you know what? It actually felt good inside. People started complimenting me ...

- "Rami, you're not trying to run off campus anymore."
- "We don't have to chase you down with security."
- "We don't have to take you to the principal's office anymore."
- "You don't have to do in-house suspensions."
- "We don't have to kick you out of in-house suspensions because you're so disruptive."

And as I moved forward, I received many positive validations because people saw the change I had made by choosing to "be good." Today, I let these kids know that when they decide to change and "be good," people are going to notice their change. People take notice more often of a person who undergoes a drastic change than someone who maybe changed more gradually or who has always remained good. You are going to make an impact on others by showing other kids they can make a change and live a better and happier life.

"Wow! You used to ditch school, you used to steal your mom's car, and you used to do drugs at the park. But now look at you. You're showing up to school and raising your grades. Good kids respect you, bad kids respect you ... everyone respects you now."

Why? Because where you once lived a life full of anger, chaos, and destruction, you made the right choice to step into a life full of peace and good decisions. As a result, you now have a new reputation you can be proud of.

For more information regarding our authors,
please visit bestsellerpublishing.org/2023anthology!

About Stephen Krempl

Stephen Krempl is the CEO of Krempl Communications International. As an international keynote speaker, trainer, and corporate communications coach, he has worked with thousands of leaders in over 30 countries. His career was spent working for Fortune 200 companies. He was chief learning officer at Starbucks Coffee Company and Yum! Brands Inc. and undertook senior learning and development roles at PepsiCo Restaurants International and Motorola. He is an expert on how leaders can stand out and get noticed in their corporations, even in an increasingly competitive global marketplace. Stephen has authored nine books, including his *Positively Negative: How to Turn Negative Messages into Positive Ones.*

His Global Executive Mindset™ and 5% Zone programs are offered through individual coaching, in-house, and online programs that focus on developing high-potential and future leaders, especially minorities, to get noticed in their organizations. The programs are based on his best-selling book *The 5% Zone: Visibility Strategies That Get You Noticed and Rewarded in any Organization.* He is now spreading this 5% message to university students to understand how to win in the working world through his W3 Accelerator program, which includes 21 online modules, an app, a book, question bank, 90-day checklist, and webinar. More information is available at the website for Winning in the Work World.

CHAPTER 9

SHOW RESILIENCE WITH THE 95/5 RULE

BY STEPHEN KREMPL

WHAT IS THE 95/5 RULE?

Ann, a semiconductor industry executive, engaged me for personal coaching on having more presence and connecting with her CEO. She was going to join her CEO and two other senior executives at a conference and exhibition in Japan. She saw this as a rare opportunity (5%) to get one-on-one time with them and make a positive impression.

She said, "The first two days went by with no opportunity; now it was the morning of the third day. I came down to attend the morning sessions, and I saw my CEO standing alone, working on his cell phone in the lobby — and my immediate reaction was instinctively to turn and walk away, to avoid contact." Then she said, "I heard a voice in my head saying, 'It is time.' In that instant, Ann turned 180 degrees around and headed back to where the CEO was standing. I will let you know what happened at the end of the chapter.

Definition

The 95/5 Rule defines those points in time when
you need to stand out when in front of a critical
audience to achieve your desired results.

The 5% opportunities could be meeting a key executive or a group of individuals from an organization who are critical to your success. It could come as an opportunity when you are being considered for the final cut of presenters at the company's annual kick-off meeting, or you're on the shortlist of the vendors providing a product or service to a large organization, or an opportunity to be on a nationally syndicated TV station that would significantly boost your credibility, or at an interview for your dream job. If you combine that opportunity with preparation, focus, and communication finesse, you will have a greater probability of standing out and achieving success.

An almost-missed opportunity

A friend of mine asked me to help his son, a new employee in a prominent venture capital firm who was chosen to be one of the speakers at the annual retreat. He knew the significance of this event, as he was the youngest staff member given the opportunity.

After having a short discussion and reviewing his slides, I knew he had an excellent story and content to get everyone's attention. When I finished sharing my thoughts, he started to walk back his idea and the efficacy of his slides, and he was wondering if the interaction I had suggested was necessary.

So I told him in a firm but friendly way, "John, here is what you should do in the opening and closing of your five-minute presentation." (That was the amount of time he had.) "Please feel free to use it; otherwise, you can stick to your original ideas."

I did not hear from him for two weeks; then I got a text saying, "Stephen, can I buy you dinner? Your ideas worked so well, and my presentation was a hit at the meeting, as I was so different from the others." What if he had gone back to his original ideas? Would it have worked as well? I couldn't say, but I think not.

How will you show up if one of those critical 5% opportunities appears before you? How much input or advice would you take from others with more experience than you? Would you be willing to try something new, or do you go for your tested and safe ways? Are you going to turn away or turn toward their advice or new ideas for your opportunity? Sometimes it is about making the small changes that could result in a huge impact.

WHY IS THE 95/5 RULE IMPORTANT?

Why the 95/5 Rule, Stephen? Well, these are the types of events that don't happen very often but are pivotal to your future. It is taking the 80/20 Rule to the next level. This is 20% of the 20 in the 80/20 Rule. The ones you can't afford to get wrong or, put more positively, the ones you want to get right.

Here are just a few of these situations:

- Corporate leader — Present your new idea to your executive team or the CEO.

- Business executive — To a brand-new client, pitch your idea which, if successful, could double your business in the next year.

- R & D — Sell that new product idea for the next big breakthrough to the marketing team.

- Sales — Land that new marquee client who will change everyone's perception of your organization in a way that no one else could do.

- Entrepreneur — Convince a qualified investor (or *Shark Tank* members) to believe in your dream and invest in your idea.

- Interviewee — Do spectacularly in the interview for your dream job.

How you behave in these 5% situations is very different from how you behave in your usual 95% of cases. Here you must put your best foot forward; otherwise, you may miss the boat and, for some, this could cause a lifetime of regret. Most of us don't get many of these opportunities. So, this article will highlight the mindset, skills, and behaviors you will need to increase your probability of success.

If you're already thinking, "Stephen, you don't understand; there are just so many things that could always go wrong or that I am not in control of," then you may already be going down a path that is not useful for you. Even worse, you may be beating yourself up when the situation does not turn out exactly the way you planned, or worse still, you're throwing in the towel too early.

THE MINDSET YOU NEED TO SHOW UP WITH

The first thing we need to do is decide if we want to be just GOOD, or be GREAT at what we do. There are more people than you can count who are GOOD at precisely what you do, but far fewer if you are looking for those who are GREAT.

However, we all know the great ones put in the preparation and work it takes to be great. Are you willing to do so? Let's say your answer is yes — then how visible, confident, and engaging are you when it comes to making an impression on your 5% audience? And when you leave the room or are not present in front of them, what do they really say about you? Do you know?

Remember, there are probably only five situations where your 5% audience will recall their encounter with you: the one-on-one meeting, the last team meeting, the virtual or conference call, the presentation, or the social encounter they had with you. Did you create a positive impression or something memorable?

To be effective in these situations, you will need to switch from your usual modus operandi to what you need to do to be effective in your 5% situations. Now, many people at this point say, "Stephen, that is not being authentic. I have been told to be 100% authentic to myself." Yes, please be authentic, but here is the clarification and nuance in the 95/5 Rule — you need to be authentic within your role.

You see, we all play different roles at different times, and we behave differently in each of them. Let's explore a few common examples:

when leading an office review meeting, you act one way; while having drinks and recalling good old times with your school buddies, you will probably act differently. If you had to meet your very traditional in-laws, you might have to adjust how you behave at dinner, and if you went to a place of worship, I believe you would act a little differently there as well. So, you behaved according to your role: a leader, a friend, a son- or daughter-in-law, or a follower of some faith.

When you interact with your 5% target audience, how can you behave and communicate with them in a way that will make you memorable?

Most of my coaching sessions usually have a practice component for individuals. Intellectually they all get what they are going to do or what they are planning to say, but here is where it breaks down. If they don't actually practice beforehand, most will stumble through or perform sub-optimally. So, practicing with someone who is on your side and whom you respect is crucial to receiving honest feedback.

Sometimes people tell me, "Well, Stephen, I get feedback from those 5% groups, and they like me." So, what I ask people to do is to try to find out exactly what the group feels. Saying you got feedback without verification is like the salesperson who was trying to sell me something that I hated, and yet I responded, "That's really good. I love it; let me think about it." In my mind, I am thinking, *I need to get out of here* — quick, polite words of praise, and then exit stage left.

Now, I know your situation may not be like that; however, how sure are you that your target audience is telling you the truth about what they really feel regarding how you came across? So, getting the correct feedback and coaching and ensuring you are on top of the feedback are paramount.

WHAT SKILLS DO I NEED SPECIFICALLY?

One could probably improve a whole host of skills, so let's use a familiar formula that will focus you on a vital few: $E = MC^2$.

Well, it is not the theory of relativity for how you show up. However, it covers all the elements I want to discuss in a way you can easily remember.

E = Energy. the same as in Einstein's formula, but most people are not even thinking about this element that they can easily control. How much energy do you put out for a particular point you are making, for your presentation or pitch, or for a discussion?

And it is not necessarily the more, the better. Yes, some of you are not putting out enough energy, but I recently witnessed a keynote address by an individual who was so over the top that we felt they were overdoing it and sounded totally fake.

M = Message. Are you clear, concise, and on point for each of your audiences?

This should be obvious to most, but I am always helping individuals hone down their long, drawn-out responses to simple questions or points they are trying to make.

Remember, a two-hour meeting is very different in the amount of detail and length you need to get your arguments across than a fifteen-minute time block.

And determining the depth and detail that you will need to give or not provide is vital. Remember, what your audience wants to hear is as (if not more) important as what you want to share with them. Do you know the right balance?

C^2 = Communicates confidently. How confident do you look and sound to your audience? Are you measured, loud enough to be heard, and focused on the audience? How do you carry yourself physically? What is your energy level? Your tone? How do you emphasize key points that the audience needs to hear?

This is not only about practice making perfect; it is about perfect practice makes perfect. Actually, it is more than that: it is perfect practice with feedback that makes perfect.

I remember a time when I was helping a client who had to do a ten-minute presentation to his CEO and, without exaggeration, we took four and a half hours going through his ten slides. Some of you are thinking, "Wow, that guy must not be very good." But are you missing the point that he really wanted to nail everything so that he would come across as GREAT in front of his CEO?

So, practice seems to be an essential element of delivering something effortlessly. When you see a Steve Jobs presentation, Steph Curry's three-pointer, or Tom Brady's 50-yard touchdown pass, you know they practiced and practiced until everyone thought they were "naturally" gifted. Yes, they had base talent, but talent alone doesn't make you GREAT.

The critical question for you is this: How much practice are you putting in for your 5% situations? First, I assume you got everything else done — your idea, your product, your process for delivering your product, and your credibility. Now we need your performance to seal the deal.

BACK TO ANN'S STORY ...

After turning around, Ann went up to her CEO and executed the plan she had practiced: to be engaging and show him her value within the organization. Later, she sent me a WhatsApp message that read, "Can I have a quick call with you? I just spoke with my CEO — we spent three hours talking. Thank you so much, and I want to tell you how it went."

When your next 5% situation appears, will you be ready, focused, and memorable?

About Angela Leapua

 Living a happy, healthy life can seem harder than ever to accomplish these days. Angela Leapua's best-selling book *Coping with Chaos: Overcoming Stress and Anxiety* will help readers pinpoint and break through their barriers to happiness. Angela Leapua is an international best-selling author, speaker, and inspiring transformational leader. Her diverse education and free-spirited, uplifting personality have pushed her to the upper ranks of health and life coaching.

Angela has a master's degree in education and business, along with doctorate-level courses in organizational leadership and management. She is a graduate of IIN in nutritional health coaching and has continued her life-coaching education through Tony Robbins's training and other recognized programs. From the corporate boardrooms to the classroom, she has coached all age groups in various topics. She is a true master teacher of life skills.

Angela Leapua's *Coping with Chaos* tackles the issues that contribute to a person's sadness, addictions, lack of motivation, and poor lifestyle choices. This book helps people recognize chaotic patterns, cope more effectively with the various forms of change, get to the root of personal problems, discover easy healthy habits, and develop new strategies for tackling challenging obstacles that are barriers to happiness.

Coping with Chaos is a down-to-earth book with practical instructions. Definitions, examples, and step-by-step guidelines will help people overcome the physical, mental, and emotional symptoms of stress and anxiety. This book will empower readers to find balance and purpose in their relationships, work, and lifestyles.

CHAPTER 10:

FIND RESILIENCE IN ANXIETY

BY ANGELA LEAPUA

I am Angela Leapua. I am an educator, international best-selling author, health/life coach, motivational speaker, and inspiring transformational leader. My mission is to help individuals break down barriers to happiness. These barriers consist of fear, stress, insecurities, anger, resentment, health issues, and overall boundaries that keep them trapped in a big black box of darkness.

I found my love of teaching healthy lifestyles while living in Hawaii for 20 years. While educating eighth graders, I realized how important a healthy lifestyle is, even at a young age. Along with teaching English, Business, Careers, and Computer classes, I wanted to teach individuals about life's purpose and healthy living. I am now able to do that.

I have been blessed to have lived in and traveled to many different places. I've realized that everyone has a story and different struggles and lifestyles. The one constant within each person's life is the fact that we all have dreams. We all dream of a perfect, happy, healthy life. The problem is, most people do not know how to achieve it. This is where my skills and experience come into play. I am privileged, thrilled, and blessed to continue my path of guiding others toward their dreams.

Along with a Health and Life-Coaching Certificate, I also have a master's degree and doctorate-level courses in education and business. I have over 20 years of experience in career planning, leadership training, family counseling, addiction recovery, and nutritional fitness. This mix of skills allows me to help guide individuals and families through life's transitions.

I was inspired to write this chapter about coping skills for overcoming stress for two reasons:

1. In the past, I too experienced high anxiety while dealing with life's challenging changes, as well as my own struggles.

2. I knew I could help others overcome their struggles and live a healthier life.

Over the past few years, I've found myself having to restructure my career, and I did not have a clear set of goals. I was feeling unstable, even a bit flighty. I found myself experiencing health issues and feeling anxious and sad. I was unable to make decisions and struggled with adapting to last-minute changes.

As I looked around and spoke to friends and family, I realized I wasn't alone in my anxiety, fears, or frustrations of the unknown. But I also noticed that I was handling my life crisis better than others were. As I reflected on my life, I realized that the coping skills I had developed as a child were stronger than those of many others. Thus, I began to research coping skills for stress management. I began to understand that worry causes stress, and stress causes anxiety. I thought, *How simple it all seems*. One thing led to another ...

IN THE FACE OF CHAOS

Do you feel like you're living in a world of chaos and uncertainty? Do you find yourself feeling anxious, stressed, irritated, lonely, sad, or confused? Do you wake up feeling overwhelmed or unsure, not knowing what the next day might bring? Do you ever feel isolated and alone?

Well, you're not alone.

Believe it or not, we're living in a very chaotic world. The year 2020 ensured that the word *chaos* became a part of our everyday vocabulary. As new challenges and uncertainties emerge, the level of an individual's stress rises. Over the course of my research I was surprised to find that a large number of Americans have blamed stress on physical health conditions — like lack of sleep, panic attacks, foggy mind, lack of motivation, and heart disease.

Fear and uncertainty have led many to experience worry, stress, and anxiety at high levels. Dealing with unforeseen changes has many questioning how to deal with everyday life. Whether it be finding a new job, adhering to new company policies, struggling because of a lack of money, becoming a homeschooling parent, or experiencing the loss of a loved one — we all need coping skills to handle and push through changes in life.

When one thinks of complete confusion and total disorder, the word *chaos* comes to mind easily. We all experience chaotic moments within our lives, but some of us naturally handle these moments better than others. Some of us express our difficulty with chaos very well. We scream, yell, throw things, and have complete meltdowns. Others hide their emotions and try to diminish the chaos by saying, "I'm fine. Just having a bad day," or "Things aren't going well lately." But if we sit back and take a good look, moments of chaos do, in fact, surround us. Each of us just handles them a little differently.

The worldwide coronavirus pandemic caused overwhelming uncertainty and instability in every aspect of daily life. Nearly everyone in the world can now say they've encountered some sort of chaos in their life. This heightened time of uncertainty has kept many people on edge, questioning what tomorrow will bring. These negative emotions can cause one to have severe health and mental issues. Learning how to deal with chaos and uncertainty in healthy ways will not only help you get through the day-to-day struggles, but also create a less stressful life.

If we consider the fact that worry causes stress and stress causes anxiety, our first thought might be *We all worry, but that doesn't mean we are all experiencing stress.* I would agree. Therefore, it is highly important for each person to be aware of their lifestyle and how they deal with a crisis. We are all going to encounter a time when we have no control of the outcome. But if someone has mastered good coping skills, they can avoid the cycle of stress and tackle the situation in a positive manner.

Coping is the method a person uses to deal with stressful situations. These may help a person face a situation, act, or be flexible and persistent in the problem-solving process. These skills can be both physical and nonphysical. Coping skills also help us to release emotions. In the process of coping with stress, a person consciously attempts to master, minimize, or tolerate stressors and problems in their life.

Everyone is naturally equipped with different coping skills. These skills are developed over time as we go through life experiences. Beginning as children, we're exposed to many different stressful situations that we have no control over. Unfortunately, we often develop undesirable and ineffective ways of dealing with these stressful mishaps. As children, we are conditioned by our parents and surroundings in either a negative or positive way.

Many of us develop methods of managing stress that will come to hinder our ability to cope with situations appropriately. It can often take years to relearn how to cope properly. As we grow and mature, these coping skills become better developed. A person's coping ability and strategic choices are also dependent upon factors such as their personality, culture, and gender. Not developing appropriate coping skills can often lead people to developing defense mechanisms to protect themselves from harm.

Worrying is the normal human response to uncertainty. As we just learned, chaos is described as uncertainty and confusion in one's life. We worry when we don't know what's going on, how to respond, or what the outcome may be. This is a sensation that everyone is familiar with and can be associated with someone becoming stressed and having high anxiety.

You've probably heard the term **stress** used in several different contexts. In this chapter, stress is defined as the mental or emotional strain you experience due to any tension-causing situation. The word *stress* is also used to describe challenges that bring about feelings of nervousness, tension, or worry. Stress is usually brought on by external forces, whereas anxiety is the internal response or reaction to stress.

Acute stress can be common and frequent but less damaging. It may arise from deadlines at work or an argument. **Episodic stress** usually means having acute stress while living a chaotic life. A person who has a type A personality or who is considered a worrier is usually in this group. The third form of stress is **chronic**. This is the most harmful form and arises from childhood traumas and long-term stress. There is an actual change in the hardwiring of the neurobiology of the brain that is associated with long-term stress.

Anxiety can be viewed as an accumulation of worry and stress. Worry is the mental or cognitive element, and stress is the biological or physical element. Anxiety is made-up stress created by our thoughts. Remember, stress is an actual threat from external forces, like change. Anxiety is the overexaggerated thoughts of what we may perceive to be true.

It can be difficult to tell the difference between stress and anxiety. Many people wonder if they can be experiencing both at the same time. We must remember that anxiety usually appears after a long period of stressful situations.

Millions of individuals experience worry, stress, and anxiety at least once in their life. Therefore, it is vital that an individual knows the warning signs and ways to relieve the pressure of worry before it turns into stress and anxiety.

Warning signs of worry, stress, and anxiety can overlap. A person may have the following symptoms: lack of sleep, weight gain or loss, mental confusion, lack of motivation, stomach pain, nervousness, nausea, headaches, and a host of other physical or mental symptoms.

There are many reasons a person may worry and experience stress. As humans, we're more like each other than we are different. Most of our worries are the same as those of our friends and family. Most people will find themselves worrying from time to time. Take comfort in the fact that others have the same concerns as you do. The main concerns are usually

- Lack of money
- Financial mismanagement
- Relationship issues (partners, family, friends, etc.)
- Failing health concerns of oneself or loved ones

- Finding life's purpose
- Questions about the future

Remember that changes often bring with them a feeling of fear, panic, or grief, followed by denial and, finally, acceptance. The good news is that there are strategies to handle changes in life. They are coping skills. There is documented research to support new ways of dealing with stress. Traditional techniques can be packaged together with new technologies. Therefore, a new way to learn coping skills is available.

When we worry, we inevitably turn to one or more coping mechanisms. These behaviors can be harmful, neutral, or helpful. We learn coping skills as a child; some learn more skills than others. A person who has had a rough life has had to tackle more challenges than a person who has had it easy. This person may have better coping skills. These behaviors may consist of

- Exercise
- Connecting with friends or family who are positive and uplifting
- Meditation
- Prayer
- Sleep

Meanwhile, negative coping behaviors include isolation, drug and alcohol abuse, overeating, and outbursts of anger.

> If a problem is fixable, if a situation is such that you can
> do something about it, then there is no need to worry. If
> it's not fixable, then there is no help in worrying. There
> is no benefit in worrying whatsoever.
> — the 14th Dalai Lama

Regardless of your personality, mental fortitude, or good fortune, something will eventually happen that triggers worry. It's inevitable. While you can't completely avoid worry, you can choose your reaction. You cannot control when chaos and uncertainty will occur, but you can control how you react to it. Developing positive coping skills and recognizing when there is a problem is the first step to easing your mind.

A positive mindset and the assurance that you have the power to rise above any challenge will almost always guarantee less worry, stress, and anxiety in your life.

About Dr. Marcia Hunter

Dr. Marcia Hunter is the author of *Communication Keys* and the Amazon #1 bestseller and international bestseller *Dream Achievement: The 6 Step Plan to an Inspired Life and Meaningful Success*. She is also coauthor of the Amazon #1 bestsellers *Success Chronicles Volume 1: You Define Your Own Success* and *Success Chronicles Volume 2: #GoalCrusher*.

With a master's degree in counseling psychology and a doctoral degree in instruction and curriculum leadership, she draws on 30 years as a psychology professor and trainer providing training and coaching — including training for Fortune 500 companies. She has also served for over ten years as a director and therapist in mental health services, a life coach, and a keynote speaker. In 2022 she was chosen and showcased as one of *SUCCESS* magazine's SUCCESS 125 leaders who help others reach their potential. In March 2023 she was again featured in *SUCCESS* magazine, highlighting her leadership as a lifelong life coach. That same month, she was featured in a *SUCCESS* magazine blog post highlighting her book *Dream Achievement*.

You may reach Dr. Marcia Hunter at her website (visit the Anthology Author Resource page for more information). You can find *Dream Achievement* (with a foreword by the notable Les Brown) on Amazon. You don't want to miss it!

For more information regarding our authors,
please visit bestsellerpublishing.org/2023anthology!

CHAPTER 11

LEADING FROM THE INSIDE
(SELF-LEADERSHIP AND SELF-DEVELOPMENT)

BY DR. MARCIA HUNTER

It is not the critic who counts; not the man who points out
how the strong man stumbles or where the doer of deeds
could have done them better. The credit belongs to the
man who is actually in the arena.
— Theodore Roosevelt

It was approaching the end of the year. My schedule was very busy. I was trying to wrap up coaching sessions with clients and close out the semester for my college students. I needed a quick diversion and break from assessments for my students and coaching clients and thus decided to spend a few minutes checking my text messages.

One of the text messages drew my attention.

Hi Dr. Hunter, this is [Pat].

I hope you remember me. I think of you often and thank God for you. You were my therapist over sixteen years ago. I will be 79 years old in a few weeks, and I have been bipolar symptom-free for sixteen years, due to the help provided by you and your treatment protocol.

I thank God for His healing power! I thank Him for you,
your love and understanding.

To protect anonymity and honor my client, I'll call her "Pat" in this article. Pat continued to give praise for my psycho-education training sessions on self-development, self-leadership, and the process of taking responsibility for her health and wellness. She indicated that the therapy and psycho-education training sessions had helped her to remain bipolar symptom-free for 16 years, despite a life of bipolar symptoms and self-sabotage from early adulthood until the time we met and began her treatment.

She expressed her appreciation and informed me that she was currently having great relationships with all her children and other family members. She ended her text message expressing love and blessings to me and my family and wishing us a very merry Christmas and a great New Year.

As indicated by the text message, this story started over 16 years before. At that time, I was serving as a mental health therapist and coach. Pat was one of my clients who suffered from a severe mood disorder. She was frequently in and out of the hospital and did not seem to be getting the results we desired. Note the pronoun *we* — I was in the arena with her, and we worked as a team. I decided to pay closer attention to her story.

She was eager to put in the work, but because her family had misunderstood her health issues for years, she was walking the recovery journey by herself. She had children and grandchildren living in close proximity to her, but owing to the stereotype of her mental health, her family members distanced themselves from her. They would not participate in family therapy or family support groups.

This lack of support affected my client's self-acceptance. She had a fair level of self-awareness about her health, but her self-acceptance was firmly fixed to her family's acceptance of her. She did not feel good enough. She was isolated from family and friends. She did not feel worthy of fighting for herself.

To break the stalemate of family support, working together we decided to invite her family to an intimate family picnic. Our intention was just to have family eating together. She decided to invite her children, who were living in close proximity, but also extended the invitation to a few family members living out of state.

The family members from out of state accepted the invitation and encouraged those living in close proximity to attend the family picnic. As a result of the fellowship at the picnic, one of the out-of-towners began asking questions about Pat's health. Having a firm sense of self-awareness regarding her health, Pat was able to answer her family's questions and put their fears at ease.

Pat's renewed acquaintance with family members increased her family's awareness as well as her self-acceptance of her own health issues. The family's acceptance and bonding also helped to enhance my client's self-awareness and further promote her self-acceptance.

Soon, my client's health improved, and she was discharged from that treatment program to a lower level of maintenance. We continued to work together, and she later was able to leave the maintenance program. She then moved out of state to be closer to the family members who had come to support her. The text I shared at the beginning of this story was her celebrating 16 years of health and joyful living. This story demonstrates the importance of self-leadership in our health and development.

SELF-LEADERSHIP

To lead is to provide guidance and influence for other people's actions and processes. For self-development, you are often encouraged to be leaders, not mere followers. However, you cannot be effective leaders of others until you can effectively lead yourself. Therefore, self-leadership is an important aspect of effective leadership.

Self-leadership occurs when you intentionally exert effort to influence your personal thoughts, feelings, and actions. I think of effective self-leadership as being in your own life arena, being in the thick of things, and providing influence and guidance to yourself from the inside out. Self-leadership requires taking responsibility for your own thoughts, attitudes, and behaviors and for the products of such thoughts, attitudes, and behaviors. Self-leadership allows us to intentionally be the CEO of our own life.

ELEMENTS OF SELF-LEADERSHIP

Key elements of self-leadership are self-awareness, self-acceptance, and self-management. Self-awareness relates to how you view yourself.

Are you aware of your strengths and weaknesses? Are you aware of your internal vibrations (such as your mindset, self-talk, attitude, and perceptions)?

Self-awareness requires honesty and self-reflection. It also requires that you are aware of your external behaviors and actions. In addition, self-awareness also dictates that you are conscious of your personal life-directed story. What is your why for living? Is it strong enough to provide the boost you desire and need to live a self-fulfilling life?

Effective leaders have a story that boosts their reason (why) for leadership. Understanding your story and its why for self-leadership will provide support when the current of life seems to be going against you. My client Pat's why for her self-leadership story was to demonstrate to herself that she can lead a healthy life and help others with a similar diagnosis lead healthy lives. Her self-awareness helped her to understand the ups and downs of her mood swings, triggers for these mood swings, and strategies that work for her to stabilize her mood.

Self-acceptance indicates that you accept yourself for who you are, but you are willing to work to grow into your most desirable self. You believe in your own possibilities, and you serve as your own cheerleader. Self-acceptance enhances resilience to negative criticism and reinforces that you are a work in progress and thus gives you permission and grace to push forward.

Pat has learned that failing is not falling. Instead, it is remaining where you fall. She now lives a life of diligent work, rest breaks, and pushing through with grace. Her self-awareness allows her not to have the desire to compare herself to others. She is aware that she is her own authentic person with self-confidence to gracefully stand alone, if and when she needs to do so.

Self-management requires you to accept the responsibility of being the CEO of your life. You are committed to work on a system of checks and balances to maintain order and growth in your life. To be an effective self-leader you need to first learn to be attuned to yourself. Be aware of your patterns of thinking.

Work to improve your belief system, and move from pessimism to optimism and from a negative and fixed mindset to a growth mindset. Replace negative self-talk with new and improved positive self-talk scripts. Your beliefs function as a mental map and direct your life. To lead and manage your life you must manage your belief system, as you are the product of your thoughts and belief system. It is said that your external world reflects your internal world. So, as a self-leader you lead from the inside out.

ATTRIBUTES OF EFFECTIVE SELF-LEADERSHIP

1. **Accomplishment of meaningful, manageable goals.** Adhering to the concept of self-development, self-leadership demands positive change, growth, and movement from your comfort zone. Establishing manageable self-leadership goals will allow you to break your goals into meaningful units. This promotes management and accomplishment of your goals and growth.

2. **Effective self-monitoring system.** Apart from establishing your goals, you need an effective self-monitoring system. This system should allow for regular monitoring and evaluation of your performance in relation to your desired goals. Growth often will not occur without appropriate support. Use support teams as a self-monitoring strategy to help raise your standards and promote success. Helen Keller is noted to have said, "Alone you can do so little. Together we can do so much."

3. **The use of personal examples.** Leadership is best demonstrated in the lives of the leaders. Self-leadership does not promote the idea of "Do as I say, not as I do." It is demonstrated in what is said as well as in what is done. Self-leadership is a lifestyle concept.

4. **Effective communication.** Self-leadership requires effective communication to ensure engagement and influence. Effective communication is important for understanding others and for being understood. Self-leadership promotes open and authentic communication for personal and professional growth.

5. **Strengths and weaknesses focus.** Self-leadership promotes diligence and consistency to enhance success. It recognizes the awareness of strengths as well as weaknesses in personal development. It promotes support to improve weaknesses and to enhance strengths. It is not viewed as a destination spot but as a measure of daily process.

6. **Accurate practice.** The concept of "practice makes perfect" is inaccurate. Only accurate and purposeful practice leads to perfect or near-perfect performance. Self-leadership requires that you should not delay progress by waiting for a perfect performance when a good performance can effectively accomplish the task at hand. Never let the desire for perfection delay your job progress and accomplishment, as what is considered perfect today may not be tomorrow.

For Pat, she had some good progress in her life and in raising her children. However, she did not take credit for her good work even though her children were productive citizens in society. She complained about and belittled herself, trying to gain perfection.

Like many of us, Pat experienced areas of self-sabotage until she learned the needed self-leadership skills. She then realized that knowledge has no power, but applied knowledge, even in small measure, leads to power. We all should adhere to the self-leadership goal of being the best version of ourselves under the umbrella of grace and love. Keep in mind the saying "Nothing works unless you work it." You are the author of your story, the CEO of your life.

★ ★ ★ ★ ★

About Amir Baluch, MD

Amir Baluch, MD, is a physician, entrepreneur, and investor based in Dallas, Texas. He is the founder and CEO of two companies:

- Baluch Capital, a wealth management platform that helps clients achieve their financial goals
- Baluch Brothers Development, a real estate development company that specializes in the construction of affordable housing

Dr. Baluch also educates his peers on personal finance and investments through his podcast, *Financial Wellness MD*.

You can find his best-selling book on Amazon: *Make It, Keep It: The New Rules of Wealth Preservation for Doctors*.

For more information regarding our authors,
please visit bestsellerpublishing.org/2023anthology!

CHAPTER 12:

THE RESILIENT JOURNEY
(NAVIGATING LIFE THROUGH THE
FOUR PILLARS OF SUCCESS)

BY AMIR BALUCH, MD

In 2001, I experienced my greatest life setback: a crushing rejection from medical school. This shook my world, as becoming a physician was my singular career focus. This devastating blow left me lost and uncertain about my future.

Before I could chart a new course, another blow landed. My father, also a physician, declared bankruptcy. Poor financial planning and over-leveraged investments had caused his financial collapse, devastating our family's stability. We were forced to sell everything and move into a small one-bedroom apartment, costing us a mere $250 per month. It was at this point that I made a promise to myself: I would never let this happen again.

SWEET CLARITY
(UNVEILING THE FOUR PILLARS OF SUCCESS)

During these challenging times, I had ample time for introspection. Staring at the ceiling fan in our humble apartment, I pondered my missteps and contemplated my next move. I was at a crossroads, tempted to give up.

After a string of odd jobs — from an EMT to a librarian to a personal trainer — and a year of soul-searching, a moment of clarity struck me. I decided to reapply to medical school and deepen my understanding of personal finance. This period of my life, while harsh, was a school in itself. Out of this "street knowledge" I distilled four key principles that became my guideposts to success: Mentorship, Ikigai, Teamwork, and Self-Awareness.

MENTORSHIP
(THE GUIDING LIGHT TO SUCCESS)

The first cornerstone of success is mentorship, an invaluable treasure that charts a less rocky path toward your goals. Picture this: you're venturing into uncharted territory, a realm that tantalizes your dreams but remains elusive in its intricacies. Would you plunge headfirst into the wilderness, or would you rather have an experienced guide who's braved these terrains before?

Just as it is in the hallowed halls of medical schools and residencies, mentorship can be a beacon of guidance in any field. Rather than learning the hard way, battling through trials and errors, why not capitalize on the wisdom of someone who's been in your shoes? A mentor can steer you clear of pitfalls, offer insightful advice, and be your sounding board. They've been there, done that, and now you can ride on the coattails of their experiences.

In my journey, I've routinely enlisted consultants' expertise and immersed myself in mastermind groups for investing and real estate. The dividends have been profound, accelerating my trajectory toward business and financial goals, allowing me the flexibility of going part-time with anesthesia while still in my early 40s.

But here's the catch: not all mentorships are cut from the same cloth. Some so-called mentors may simply be entrepreneurs with coaching businesses who may not have a substantial track record of success in their chosen field. It's crucial to scrutinize their credentials, inquire about references, and make sure they've achieved what you're aspiring to.

Remember, in the quest for mentorship, you're seeking not just a teacher, but a partner in your journey toward success. Choose wisely, and the rewards will be manifold.

THE MAGIC OF IKIGAI
(DISCOVERING YOUR TRUE CALLING)

Ikigai, a Japanese concept that translates to "a reason for being," holds the key to success. This second pillar of achievement fuses together four elements: your passion, your skills, the world's needs, and your earning potential. Unearthing your ikigai can feel like striking gold; it can harmoniously align your personal and professional life, bringing fulfillment and success.

Take my journey, for instance. As a self-confessed science enthusiast, I was always fascinated by the intricacies of the human body. This passion, combined with my proficiency in the subject, guided me toward a career in medicine — a profession that's always in demand and well compensated. It became my ikigai, my purpose, my driving force.

But here's the fascinating part: I discovered that we can have more than one ikigai. As I plunged into the world of entrepreneurship, I found another arena where I could couple my passion and skills to address a need — creating businesses. The beauty of entrepreneurship is its versatility. You can build a business based on your interests and strengths, delegate tasks that don't spark joy, and still make a positive impact.

So, let's embark on this journey of self-discovery. Unlock your ikigai; find that sweet spot where your love, your talent, the world's needs, and your financial prospects intersect. Therein lies a wellspring of fulfillment and success waiting to be unleashed.

THE POWER OF TEAMWORK
(UNITED WE TRIUMPH)

Success is not a solo expedition. It's a collective journey, a chorus of harmonized efforts, a synergy of dreams and aspirations. Like pieces of a grand puzzle, each individual brings unique strengths to the table, crafting an image greater than the sum of its parts.

It's a rare spectacle to witness monumental success without a powerhouse team driving it. Just as a grand symphony requires an orchestra, a truly influential feat needs a proficient team. This profound truth forms the cornerstone of the third pillar — teamwork.

Building a dynamic, high-performing team is an art. I seek out those A players, the ones whose zest and brilliance can electrify the atmosphere. To understand these individuals better, I employ tools like DISC and Kolbe personality tests. These help me identify their strengths and weaknesses, allowing me to assign roles where they can truly shine and realize their own personal ikigai.

The entrepreneurial journey often lures us into a dangerous illusion, the mirage of "I can do it all." But a solo voyage can quickly spiral into a herculean task. When we share the load, the impossible begins to seem achievable. A unified team not only fuels your vision but also buoys your spirit during turbulent times. It amplifies your strengths and covers your blind spots, forging a collective resilience against hardships.

In essence, teamwork is the art of joining together to create beautiful symphonies from diverse notes. And when each note resonates with the team's shared vision, the symphony becomes a captivating melody of success.

SELF-AWARENESS
(THE COMPASS OF SUCCESS)

The final cornerstone of success is self-awareness. It requires a clear and honest introspection into your own capabilities, an ability to critically evaluate your strengths and, more importantly, your weaknesses. This knowledge becomes a vital tool, guiding you toward individuals whose skill sets fill the gaps in your own.

Entrepreneurs, who carry the mantle of launching and running their businesses, stand to gain the most from this pillar. Recognizing your limitations helps you in seeking and accepting the assistance required to overcome these hurdles, thereby propelling the business forward.

To illustrate, let me share a personal anecdote. Podcasting and hosting live conferences were aspects of my career that I found daunting. My voice didn't seem to resonate well in recordings, and the thought of making a blunder during a live event, where no second takes are allowed, was enough to make me apprehensive.

However, recognizing this anxiety was my first step toward resolution. I collaborated with experienced producers, whose expertise in their field boosted my confidence, infusing an element of fun into the entire process. Their assurance transformed my perspective, making these challenging tasks enjoyable.

So, embracing self-awareness is not about exposing our vulnerabilities but about converting them into stepping stones toward our goals.

BUILDING RESILIENCE ON THESE FOUR PILLARS

No great achievement comes without hard work and challenges. Business, in particular, is a tumultuous journey, filled with unpredictable ups and downs. But with the four pillars in place, you bolster your resilience, enabling you to weather the storm. Your mentors and team provide necessary support, while your ikigai fuels your passion to keep pushing forward.

Remember, there are no unrealistic goals, only unrealistic timelines. Perseverance guarantees that you inch closer to your goals. My most successful mentors and business partners have all encountered seemingly insurmountable obstacles, but their unwavering resolve to keep moving ensured their eventual success. This mindset can be applied to any aspect of life — business, relationships, health, or spiritual growth.

Looking back, the events that I once perceived as catastrophic failures were blessings in disguise. They provided me with the resilience needed to pursue my dreams and instilled in me a passion for reaching my goals. Eventually, I did get accepted into medical school, paving my way to become an anesthesiologist.

Due to the resilience I built upon these four pillars, I achieved my dreams and ensured my parents could retire comfortably. It was this resilience that saw me through my journey as an entrepreneur and investor, despite numerous challenges. The promise I made to myself in that one-bedroom apartment served as a constant reminder of my determination to build multiple streams of income and secure financial stability.

Today, my journey stands as a testament to the power of resilience, hard work, and determination. Never once did I entertain the thought of giving up on my dreams. I soldiered on, continuously learning and growing, eventually carving out a successful career as an entrepreneur and investor.

About Dr. Gena Lester

 Dr. Gena Lester is a college admissions expert, speaker, business coach, and *Wall Street Journal* and *USA Today* best-selling author. She has guided families through education and college admissions for over 25 years. Additionally, she works with entrepreneurs to grow their businesses by adding online systems that scale.

Being widowed at a young age, she knows all too well that tomorrow is not promised. It was because of her experience that she set out to design a business that gave her the freedom to live life to the fullest, never miss a moment with her loved ones, and run a successful business. She was able to achieve her dream and now runs a multi-six-figure business from anywhere in the world on her own schedule. She loves sharing her systems and processes with others so they can reach their goals.

Her background is in both education and psychology and includes a double master's in higher education and in industrial and organizational psychology, as well as a PhD and doctorate. Dr. Lester developed the U-Niquely-U™ formula, which she uses to help teens get into the college of their dreams and to help entrepreneurs find their passions and be more successful on their journey.

For more information regarding our authors,
please visit bestsellerpublishing.org/2023anthology!

CHAPTER 13:

NEW BRICKS, NEW MORTAR
(THE MODERN MODEL FOR TRANSITIONING YOUR
BUSINESS ONLINE AND YOUR LIFE INTO FREEDOM)

BY DR. GENA LESTER

Being a business owner is something that many people dream of. The idea of leaving that 9-to-5 job so you are not tied to someone else's ideas and restrictions is glorious. In our minds we see financial freedom, we see time freedom, and we have the idea that we are going to create this amazing lifestyle. What we don't see is that many times we are trading hours for dollars, and we go from a 9-to-5 job to a 6 a.m.-to-midnight job. The financial pressures of operating expenses and employees leave us with little in our pockets. Did you know that the average small business with employees will last only two years, or that it can take two or three years for a business to be profitable?

I am one of the fortunate ones in that I began making a profit in the first few months of my business. I was the bootstrap queen. But I was trading time for dollars. I woke up early and went to bed late. At the time, my husband was in the late stages of Parkinson's disease. He was in a nursing home, and our youngest daughter had just left for college. So, throwing myself into work allowed me to be there for my husband while giving myself purpose. The problem was that after my husband passed away, my lifestyle did not change. The long hours and the stress of growing my business weighed heavily on me. My friends and family often commented on the fact that I was always working. But my story is not all sad; an amazing man, who was also a widow, came into my life. I was able to find love a second time. During that time, I began pulling back and working a little less to spend time with my new husband, but I found that my business began to suffer.

ONLINE NOISE
(CREATING SPACE AND SYSTEMS)

The harsh reality was that my business was running me instead of me running my business. It was not fun; while I loved working with the students and seeing their success, it all came at a cost. I did not want to wake up one day and realize that I was at the end of my life and had missed out on making memories with the ones I love or experiencing life in a joyful, fun way. I am an entrepreneur at heart; therefore, I went into problem-solving mode. Not to spoil the surprise, but I was able to create a new business structure that changed my life and allowed me to 10x my business in 2020. The best part is that I am running my business now, instead of it running me, and I am in control of my schedule and hours.

To go from point A to point B, we need to do a deep dive into where you are today. If you are a consultant, coach, counselor, or other business professional who is the expert and who works with clients in a 1:1 setting, I want to challenge you to have an open mind and consider possibilities outside of the traditional. What did I do, you ask? I created an online system that allows me to work from any corner of the world. I am sure that at this point you are thinking, "In our new COVID world we are all seeing clients online," or, "I see all the online noise out there and my clients want to meet with me; this is just not going to work for my business or industry." I am here to challenge that thought. When I decided to move into the online space, I was working with teens, so I had to sell my product to the parents and convince them that their kids would be successful online and would get the value they were paying for. No one in my industry was doing this. And believe me, there were many in my industry who said it would never work or that it could not be done.

Mindshift
(Shut out the noise)

The first thing I would challenge you with is to shut out all the noise. You are not going to throw out the baby with the bathwater. I did not call my clients and say, "Sorry, guys, no more 1:1 meetings ..." Instead, I began thinking about my customer's journey from a different perspective. In my industry, a majority of our clients are from families in high-income brackets; their kids are academically strong, and the parents are professionals who understand the value of getting an education from an "elite" university.

Going into research mode, I found that there were many families who wanted the same opportunities for their kids but did not realize that our industry existed and could not afford to pay for private college consulting. A secondary group were families of students whose parents had not attended college in the U.S. and had no idea how to navigate the system. These families were online, trying to find every nugget of information that they could, searching Facebook, Instagram, YouTube, LinkedIn, or Reddit. And while there were articles and posts, it would take hours of searching to find the needed info. Many families would say to me that it was a full-time job trying to help their teen, and still many of them were not as successful as they could have been if they had the resources they needed.

With this knowledge, my next step was to consider how I could create a business model that appealed to this group of families. The first thing I did was to create a group-coaching program that was high touch but more affordable for families. I took my 1:1 meeting and it became 1:30 per group. This one move allowed me to triple my income overnight. I went from 30 hours a week, seeing students 1:1, to 1 hour a week in my groups. My success rate did not change; the students were getting into all the top-ranking colleges and having greater success in some ways. From there I added DIY courses, mini-workshops, a parent membership, plug-and-play resources, and templates. Families can now find resources that fit their budget and help their teens achieve their dreams, and I am able to impact future generations.

Worldshift
(Environment, needs, and services)

Since making the shift in my business, I have become a trendsetter in my industry and for other professionals who work 1:1 with clients. The exciting thing is that it has allowed me to expand into business coaching. I now help other professionals, coaches, consultants, counselors, and educators create a lifestyle business that gives them the freedom that they desire.

There are lots of people teaching how to create a course or how to build a membership, but as professionals I know that we have specific hurdles to overcome. You may be thinking this sounds great, but in my industry, we are required by law to (fill in the blank). And what about privacy? These are all issues that can be addressed. It is all about mindset and thinking outside the box. I see lawyers who are offering memberships for legal services and counselors who have courses on how to combat anxiety or panic. In my industry we have a code of ethics that we must adhere to in order to be in good standing with our professional organizations. I am not a lawyer, and I'm not here to give you legal advice. You must do your own due diligence to ensure that you are compliant with all regulations in your industry.

The reality is that since 2020 the world has shifted. Doctors are now seeing patients online, online education for kids has exploded, and more employees are working remotely. People are looking for flexibility. They want the freedom to accomplish and learn in an environment that fits their needs. I want to be clear that 1:1 meetings are not going away, but they should be only one component of your business.

If you are ready to make the shift but are not sure where to start, I want you to remember that Rome was not built in a day. You are a busy professional, so give yourself grace. Start small, and pick one thing that you can create that would allow you to increase your revenue but not increase your hourly workload. For me, I started with creating a group-coaching program. This took me almost a year to develop, so if you are looking for a quick win, I suggest you start somewhere else. But it was also a pivotal point for my business. Maybe you want to create a course or a workshop. The goal here is to keep the concept of "1:many" in front of you. I have created a resource for you to use that will guide you through a brainstorming exercise to help you determine the best place to start.

A Sustainable Dream

I want to end with what I hope will be inspiration for you. This is all about my personal journey. I shared earlier with you that my husband and I are both widows. We each lost our first spouse in our early 50s. We'd had dreams of retirement, travel, grandbabies, and all the things you plan for as you go through your life. This was not the reality for either of us. The one thing I have learned is that life is short and we are not promised tomorrow. As we began our lives together, we found ourselves in the same trap of stress from work, long hours, commutes for my husband, and putting our dreams off for later. We decided that my husband would retire early and come work in the business with me. We started working toward moving the business 100% remote, which would give us the freedom to travel and spend time with my aging parents and our six kids, who are all over the U.S.

By the beginning of 2021 we were able to achieve that dream. The business was more profitable than it had ever been, and the model was sustainable even if I took time off. We then sold our home, put our stuff in storage, and decided to live our dream. We currently live in and travel the country in our beautiful motor home and are able to go anywhere in the world at any time we choose. We run the business from the road, and we have not missed a beat. We are experiencing all the beauty of our country and wake up to some of the most beautiful views every morning. I get to spend weeks visiting with kids and grandkids versus holidays and weekends. But the best part is that I get to impact those who come through my business. I love what I do, and I get joy from seeing others achieve their dreams. And I did not have to choose between my passion and life.

It takes work to get to this point in your life. You have to make the commitment to step out of the norm and be willing to learn things that are new or may even feel hard, but the reward is great. The benefits of moving your business to include an online model will be worth it in the end. Take a step back and look at your business. Are you running it? Or is it running you? What do you want your business to look like? You may not want to live on the road. Maybe you want to help coach your son's soccer team or attend your kid's events without being tied to your phone. Maybe you're building toward your retirement. Wherever you are, take inventory, and use the tools I provided you with in the book to determine where you are and the best place for you to begin your online journey.

About Roger Khoury

 Roger Khoury is an expert in the field of market forecasting, with over two decades of experience.

In 2010, he developed an innovative, probability-based form of price forecasting called Market Vulnerability Analysis™ (or MVA™); MVA overcomes an inherent flaw Khoury discovered to be unavoidably baked into every trading and investment strategy developed for the world's financial markets.

This inherent flaw is the root cause of the uncertainty felt in the markets, as well as the large drawdowns and inconsistent performance results often experienced.

Khoury's proprietary form of real-time demand analysis provides its users with an unparalleled level of control over their performance outcomes, enabling them to uniquely reduce the downside risks in the market without sacrificing the upside performance potential, through the accurate risk forecasting capability his MVA™ methodology provides.

After successfully deploying his proprietary demand analysis and risk forecasting methodology (MVA™) to execute a strategy, Khoury also developed Demand Imbalance Arbitrage™ to reach his own goals, which gave him an abundance of free time. People began to inquire about his accomplishments.

Since 2011, over 90% of clients learn about and come to Khoury through word-of-mouth personal referrals from existing clients.

CHAPTER 14:

PEACEFUL PROFITS
(RETHINK GOALS AND PROFIT FOR UNPARALLELED CONTROL)

BY ROGER KHOURY

I've been a business consultant for most of my adult life. That's really what paved the way and ultimately funded my massive learning curve over the years. After building up quite a nice business, I reached a point where I felt like I'd outgrown my ability to manage everything on my own and that it was time to bring in some other talent. I took on a partner who I believed would help me grow the business to the next level.

Eventually, that partner embezzled money (and went to jail for it) and did some really horrible things that blew up 15 years of my life.

During those years, I was investing in some commodities and some projects overseas. Managing all of those details in multiple time zones was very stressful.

Still hurting from the betrayal of my former partner, I was feeling like people weren't reliable, and relying on others and letting things go that were out of my control was very frustrating for me. When I was talking to my brother one day, he leveled with me in a big way:

> You know, you're killing yourself. It's so frustrating to
> me that you keep leaning on and depending on other

people. You're trying to rebuild your life from scratch. But why don't you do something where you can have full control? You keep looking to depend on someone who agrees with you, works with you, and stays honest, loyal, and faithful.

Don't do that anymore. You need to focus where nobody's gonna derail you or compete with you. Why don't you go back and find a way to be consistent with your trading? I know you love that. I know you've been asked about that. And I'll ask again. Why don't you focus on that 100%? Why don't you stop pushing yourself into something that you can't control the outcome of? I know that you believe in God. You have faith. So why don't you pray for him to help you?

And I was like, *Such a simple thing.*

I've always been kind of driven by my own mind and by what I can do and what I can accomplish when I put my mind to it. But, in fact, I had never actually prayed for help and direction with this.

And so I prayed for help and asked God to give me guidance and illuminate my path. I would focus 100% on it.

This led to an interesting series of epiphanies and moments of transformative understanding about the financial markets that later became the foundation for what I ended up developing.

However, along the way, I hit what seemed to be yet another setback, which reinforced my feeling that I must be cursed or something.

I found myself feeling extremely angry, and the stress boiled over. I needed a reset. I dropped everything and went to the beach to calm myself down. What had seemed like a curse, though, this time around ended up being a blessing in disguise!

As I sat at the beach, I noticed a group of surfers out on the water, and I found myself starting to count them.

There were 17 surfers in all. As I watched them, I noticed that 15 out of the 17 surfers were taking on wave after wave. They'd ride for a bit and often crashed and burned.

Then I noticed the other two surfers were positioned to the side, watching the others. Every once in a while, those two would take a wave — but nowhere near as often as the other 15. And I thought, *Those two must be newbies. They must be observing and learning from the other more experienced surfers.*

But after about an hour, I became aware of an interesting pattern. Every time the two surfers took a wave, they had a great ride and it worked out really well for them.

Eventually it dawned on me that the other 15 surfers weren't the experienced pros. It was the other way around.

Because somehow, these two surfers had figured out how to identify which waves were worth taking and which ones were worth avoiding.

And, by the way, they avoided most of the waves that were available to ride.

Then, suddenly, the light bulb went on. I had an epiphany. These two guys weren't looking to catch every wave that looked like a good ride.

They were looking for a wave that was NOT likely to give them a bad ride.

Likewise, I realized that I had been acting like the inexperienced surfers in my business endeavors. My focus had been on opportunities that were likely to make money. But, instead, what I should really have been doing was focusing on opportunities that were NOT likely to lose money.

As I further reflected, my thoughts led me to a revelation that soon gave me ultimate control for generating what I call Peaceful Profits.

THE PROCESS OF GENERATING PEACEFUL PROFITS

There can be a day when you have control over your financial outcomes that's not subject to things outside your control. There can be a day when you have confidence. There can be a day when you no longer have to worry about anything or anyone competing with you, or requiring you to change your ability in order to have what you want.

On that day, you will develop a level of peace, time freedom, and security about your future that you probably didn't think was possible. It will be your sweet spot.

This is when your ambition and drive to push endlessly for more fade away and you begin to truly relax from within and genuinely relish your extra free time and enjoy your life.

Today, I guide others to that sweet spot through a different category of investing and trading the markets than what is typically offered to the masses. And when it comes to advising clients, I really try to impart two mindsets to them:

1. The pursuit of goals is not the best way to bring about the desired results.

2. Looking for seemingly profitable opportunities is the wrong focus.

The backward pursuit of goals

Honestly, I discourage my clients from trying to trade for a living.

I encourage them to use my forecasting and real-time demand analysis process and the consistency it delivers to allow a part-time investing effort to replicate their full-time income.

As they accomplish this, the idea is to then take that abundance, that continued growth, and move it into passive-income-yielding investments that then replicate a full-time income for the ultimate in time freedom.

Done as prescribed, they never *need* to trade the market. If they need it, then that's a form of pressure that'll eventually work against them, and I help them avoid that mental trap.

Instead, they trade because they *want* to, for better outcomes, more control, and the enjoyment of a healthy challenge, which keeps the mind sharp and provides them with something to do that's still productive well into retirement. It's an enhancement. They're maintaining — they're not under pressure.

When any of us engage with something financial, we want to avoid being under pressure. Pressure charges our emotions and can lead us to lose composure and objectivity.

A lot of us are very goal oriented. We think in terms of wanting to make or earn something to prove something to ourselves or others. In my life, I've learned that this becomes counterproductive very quickly.

And I know that some of you might be getting irritated and start to push back while you read this sentiment.

However, in an era of vision boarding — the challenge is to dream big!

We're told, "Go after your goals and dreams!" But I have found a pattern of inconsistency and frustration in the life of nearly everyone I've seen, impacted, counseled, and mentored by those philosophies.

So that style of thinking actually achieves the exact opposite, because it misses a critical element that's required but often overlooked. It distracts you from the true drivers of success that you really need to be focused on.

If you have a goal to make X% per month or year with your activities, from what I've experienced both within my own life as well as in the lives of the many people I've mentored, two things generally happen:

1. You're going to naturally have a narrowed field of vision and perspective, kind of like putting blinders on.

2. You're going to apply pressure to yourself.

Neither of those actually serve you. In truth, it's a form of self-sabotage.

Instead of focusing on performance, percentage, or dollars, I learned the hard way that you need to focus on a "process" that delivers reliable, repeatable, consistent results — results that can compound and deliver what you're looking for in a dependable and sustainable way.

So, I tell everyone, don't focus on what you need to make. That's stressful on many levels. Focus instead on being a good steward of the process that leads to the outcome you're intending and to generating peaceful profits.

And if your goal is to apply the process as faithfully and as properly as you can, you'll find that results are not only accomplished, but often exceed your needs and your goals.

It's the process that delivers results — not the pursuit of goals.

The blind spot of profitable opportunities

The other sentiment I share with clients is that I want them to avoid seeking opportunities that will make them money. Instead, they need to focus on opportunities that are NOT likely to lose money. Everything changes from that perspective.

First, it's important to recognize that no matter what strategy you use or develop, there's an inherent flaw that's unavoidably baked into every strategy that's designed to profit from the world's financial markets — no matter what system or time frame you pursue.

This flaw is the reason all market participants experience inconsistency, while some feel stuck putting up with large drawdowns, struggling with self-doubt and fear-based actions, among other self-sabotaging behaviors.

Every strategy or setup is developed within a certain set of conditions in a market that has certain characteristics. As conditions and seasons change in the markets (as they ALWAYS DO), the strategies naturally lose their advantage and start to produce a hit-or-miss experience.

This forces the individual to essentially go back to the drawing board to look for yet another way to make the markets work for them — looking for the next new thing that'll work now. And this cycle endlessly repeats itself.

The only remedy to stop this frustrating cycle is to have a principle-based process that transcends time, circumstance, and condition.

Principles are unchanging, so having a principle-based process means you'll no longer need to keep changing things up just to have an edge in the markets every time market conditions change and no longer favor a certain strategy.

Using the principles of demand that drive all market prices is the only way to be able to forecast the market accurately and with a sustainable range of consistency.

Once my clients learn to forecast the market accurately, they can't help but feel a sense of empowerment and confidence from their newfound clarity and consistency.

However, just because the markets are forecastable doesn't mean they are always tradeable.

In other words, it doesn't mean there's always something they'll want to engage in. There's wisdom to applying an adaptive analysis and forecasting method that never needs updating.

Most often, the market is too stormy (think higher levels of risk). You don't want to have that kind of pressure. You don't want the blinders that come with aggressive, pressure-filled behaviors. You don't want to take your eyes off the objectivity of the data.

It's too easy to begin rationalizing behaviors and actions that don't serve you. You want to stay calm, clear minded — away from pressure.

If it's 80%–90% stormy, then we want to engage only the 10%–20% of calm, peaceful action that actually gives you a peaceful, low- to no-stress experience of making profits and outperforming the markets.

It's important to shift our focus away from opportunities that are likely to make us money.

What we actually want is a process to enable us to focus on identifying — objectively and clearly — the opportunities that are not likely to lose money. This is where we can find control and stability in the long term.

I have all kinds of clients. And for the ones who don't try putting their own spin on the time-tested process — the ones who are faithful to it — I see a very specific journey. They go from having inconsistent, hit-or-miss results to outperforming their hopes and desires.

And there isn't a single person who hasn't dramatically surpassed their hopes and desires when they focus on the process while looking for opportunities that are not likely to lose money.

It gives them a tremendous amount of control, freedom, and stability — which is what people truly want.

After a few months, they realize this consistency is their new normal. It's not going to stop. And then something else happens — they experience a form of relaxation.

Some of them tell me trading has become a no-stress experience, a fun puzzle to be solved like a crossword. There is so much to gain not only by being a good steward of the process but also by shifting the focus to opportunities that are not likely to lose money.

There is freedom in having a process that delivers with reliable consistency. There is confidence, peace, and security.

RIPPLES OF GRATITUDE AND LOVE

When I originally accomplished my own goals, all of a sudden I had all this free time on my hands. I thought I would just go out, socialize, have a good time, and enjoy life.

And then an interesting event happened: my dad's health took a turn for the worse.

I started spending 10–14 hours a day, every day of the week, at my dad's bedside. I was committed to not letting him feel depressed. In essence, he was losing his will to live. It was a very difficult time. It was miserable for us as a family.

Our lives were flipped upside down. Rather than use my newfound time for me, I gave it to my dad as I supported him. And that ordeal went on for about five and a half years.

During that time, people started asking, "Would you be willing to teach me what you know?" I had a handful of hours a week when I could step into my own bubble, to mentally and emotionally get away, and share my insights and knowledge through my laptop while being by my dad during the times he napped.

It was one of the healthiest, most productive things for me because it was a bright part of my life.

I'll be honest: being with an elderly parent and taking care of them through their health challenges can suck the life out of you. It's depressing. It's really hard.

But then I would see my students and mentees steadily transform their lives. I would see what our conversations meant for their families.

There was an incredible ripple effect as I received gratitude and love. It was so uplifting. I think it saved me. Those conversations, those ripples, enabled me to get through that harsh period of five and a half years.

When people acknowledge you and are willing to value you, there is an amazing sense of accomplishment — which is fulfilling.

And of course, nobody ever wants to say no to making more money — especially when it comes in a fun, fulfilling, and rewarding way.

However, personally, there was always a sense of discomfort in taking money from people. And for many of us, when we accomplish something for ourselves, we are often too proud to accept it.

As I started sharing my knowledge with others, I was able to figure out a fee structure that I was comfortable with. I created a process in which I would not only be the good steward but also teach my students how to accomplish the same. Ultimately, I wanted to share in their success.

In exchange for my time, overhead, and resources, they would cut me in at 10% until the cost of the full predetermined tuition was covered — but only when they had actually doubled the money they'd initially invested to cover the cost of training and mentoring, which basically covers my cost to train and support them to acquire my methodology.

And then anything beyond that was all theirs. Not only that, they would now understand how to continue growing their investment in a self-reliant way. I now had an incentive in which I could invest my emotions and effort without prideful discomfort.

Whenever my newfound clients would approach me, I could just be excited. I wanted to be there. By having equity in each of their successes, it felt much more intellectually honest.

Since then, my work has continued to be such an awesome experience. My clients' spouses will call me after a year or a year and a half to tell me know how much positive change they see in their partner: "My husband is not only more patient as a person, he's so much more present with his family. He's with us, and his mind isn't elsewhere." Not only am I helping others profit with their investment, I'm also seeing personal growth.

I received such joy helping others while taking care of my father, and that kind of feedback is very gratifying. I get to have fun while carrying forward those ripples of gratitude and love. Some of my clients have become great friends.

In fact, as I write this, a client and his wife are visiting for a week so that we can spend quality time together. That's far more valuable to me than any monetary profit.

That kind of personal connection is what I thrive on. And so, in closing, I encourage you to rethink your process and pursuit of making profits. In other words, instead of focusing on the end goal, focus on having a reliable process that naturally leads to the goal (because you can control that).

And last, instead of focusing on opportunities to make money, learn how to identify the opportunities that are NOT likely to lose money. This way, you get to keep more of your money, and the opportunities you do take are consistently high-probability winners.

Those distinctions have made all the difference for me and my clients, and I'm confident they will for you as well!

★ ☆ ★ ☆ ★

ABOUT DR. DEANNE DE VRIES

 Dr. Deanne De Vries is grateful to have a career she is passionate about and that she can make a difference with in the lives she touches. She found her sweet spot over 30 years ago as a business-woman, thought leader, researcher, educator, and trusted advisor at the intersection of culture, leadership, business, and politics — particularly as it relates to Africa and the Middle East.

She founded her own firm to expand the audiences she can help to further the impactful work she is doing with global for- and non-profit organizations and investors who want to be part of Africa's growth story, helping them expand across borders and create multicultural teams.

Dr. De Vries gained extensive knowledge during a career that spanned five continents, and she now shares this knowledge through her international best-selling books *Africa: Open for Business*, which was voted Best Africa Business Book of the Year 2023, and *Africa: Reframing Political Leadership* (available on Amazon).

She's even more excited that her books are starting to be used in university curricula, as her passion is to share with and inspire young people to discover what she loves to call AfriCAN — the can-do continent — and inspire them to take up the mantle of public service.

For more information regarding our authors,
please visit bestsellerpublishing.org/2023anthology!

CHAPTER 15

THE KEY TO GLOBAL GROWTH
(REFRAMING RESILIENCE THROUGH THE LENS OF CULTURE AND CONTEXT)

BY DR. DEANNE DE VRIES

When I was growing up in California, earthquakes were a common occurrence. As I sat in my high school French class, the teacher had just handed out our test papers when an earthquake struck. The German and Indian foreign exchange students started screaming and ran out of the classroom, jumping over the hedges into the middle of the parking lot, looking absolutely terrified.

The rest of us? We just remained at our desks, unfazed. We were completely unaware that growing up in California made us resilient to earthquakes.

RESILIENCE THROUGH THE AGES

The word *resilience* has gone from its Latin origins (the verb *resilire* means to rebound or recoil) to describing the durability of British naval ships and ecological systems, to becoming a rallying cry for sustainability, to measuring the impact of trauma on children, to preparing American soldiers for the VUCA world — volatile, uncertain, complex, ambiguous.

Today, *resilience* is a buzz word used so frequently by corporations, consultants, and bloggers that it risks becoming seen as simply "the flavor of the month."

Tremendous work has gone into studying resilience. However, most research is based on a handful of countries from North America and Europe that comprise just 15% of the world's population and have an above-average economic and educational level and a substantially above-average income. This means that our understanding of resilience among the majority of countries and 85% of the globe's population is quite limited. Yet, as we'll see below, without framing resilience within culture and context, its meaning is out of touch at best and irrelevant at worst.

I experienced this firsthand when I moved to Africa and came face to face with situations that my life, up to that point, had not prepared me for. I love languages, and at the time I first landed in Africa, in Kenya, I was fluent in five. But Kenya has over 30 languages, and I spoke only one of them — English.

When I look back, what first seemed overwhelming is now second nature. I quickly learned Swahili and a smattering of many local languages, which ensured I was never overcharged in the market or on the *matatus* (public minivans). With each year I spent in Africa, I grew in my understanding of people's cultures and the context of their lives.

Today, understanding local business environments, sourcing accurate statistics, and knowing the protocol for ministerial or presidential meetings all come naturally. What 30 years ago first seemed to me to be incongruous and impossible to overcome, I now don't blink an eye at. I smile when people tell me that I must be very resilient to have lived in and worked across Africa for so many years. The truth is, each one of us develops resilience in accordance with the always-changing context of our lives.

THE IMPORTANCE OF CONTEXT TO RESILIENCE

Resilience is viewed, experienced, and developed via the lenses through which we view the world: culture, society, government, faith, and race.

Resilience is influenced by history, personal experiences, socio-economics, education, morals, and family. Just like growing up in the context of California had made earthquakes "normal" to me, so too had living in Africa become normal to me. I didn't think I was resilient; it was just normal everyday life.

How would you rank the following countries in terms of their resilience? Afghanistan, Chile, France, Iraq, Mozambique, New Zealand, and the U.S.

To answer that, you'd first need to "walk a mile in their shoes" to understand the context within which people there live their daily lives. For example, many Afghans have learned to live in the face of hardships few elsewhere in the world can imagine. Dr. Catherine Panter-Brick, who has studied resilience to war in Afghanistan and famine in Niger, describes the resilience of Afghan families in one word: hope.

She elaborated that "in my work, I found that Afghan families believe that the future matters much more than the past in determining their present well-being: being able to get up each day and go harness resources toward securing a better future, matters more than the turmoil and traumas of the past."[5]

Those living in the U.S. have a very different context to their lives, which has informed their resilience. However, the growing polarization of society, regular race-based attacks, and continual killing of innocent children and adults by guns are all changing the fabric and context of Americans' lives — and along with it, what it means to be resilient in America.

Mozambique, on the southeastern coast of the continent of Africa, provides yet another context within which to view resilience. Its residents have been dealing with insurgencies in the northern part of the country and have had five severe cyclones in five years in the country's east and central parts. Yet like the Timex watch, they continue to "keep on ticking," earning a living, and raising families.

---

5. Southwick, S. M., Bonanno, G. A., Masten, A. S., Panter-Brick, C. & Yehuda, R. (2014) Resilience definitions, theory, and challenges: interdisciplinary perspectives. *European Journal of Psychotraumatology*.

Context is also important when we look at the resilience of individuals. Which of the following people would you describe as resilient?

- The pilot Sully Sullenberger, landing a plane on the Hudson River

- The widow in a refugee camp in Kenya, raising and feeding her three children

- The office worker, meeting deadlines while working from home during COVID

- The individual asked by his political, military, and religious peers to take on the role of president and help his country transition to civilian leadership

- The athletes competing in the Olympics

- The entrepreneur in Kenya, developing special gloves and an app so he can communicate with his deaf niece

Each of those individuals displays great resilience in their situation, in their particular field. Each one has developed their resilience within a specific context. Some have studied or trained for years; others have had situations forced upon them with no advance warning. All display resilience.

An awareness of context allows for a more relevant definition and understanding of resilience. So does an appreciation of culture.

CULTURAL RESILIENCE

You have seen the headlines that go something like this:

- Home Depot pulls out of China, failing to inspire DIY trend

- Starbucks flounders in Australia; drinks too hot and too expensive

- Woolworths exits Nigeria

- Unable to adapt to the local business environment, Walmart creeps out German consumers with their greeters

- Coors translation mishap sends a very wrong message to Spanish consumers

- ShopRite exits Uganda; can't beat out local competition

In their home markets, these companies displayed resilience. They were able to navigate recessions, supply-chain challenges, competition, and more. What happened?

In my 30 years of working for and advising companies as they expand into new markets, I have heard too many say, "We have a product [or service] and money; we are ready to expand." A year or two later, these same companies are exiting those same markets with their tails between their legs. Why?

They lacked resilience because they showed little interest in or respect for the local culture — that same culture that informs how business is done, what their employees' work ethics are, how leaders are viewed, how consumers view or use products, and more.

Let's look at two specific ways culture can build your resilience when you expand into new markets. We'll compare and contrast two cultural perspectives between African and Western cultures: community and wealth.

Community versus individualism

Across Africa, community, referred to as *Ubuntu* (Zulu), *Ujamaa* (Swahili) or *Omenala* (Igbo), is the source of one's belonging and values. It signifies togetherness and interdependence, teamwork, mutual respect, and a participative way of working and decision-making.

This differs considerably from the Western focus on individuality, where people are encouraged and expected to be independent and where personal success is valued more highly than group success or group achievement.

When hard times come, Africans reach out to the neighbors and friends in their communities whom they see and interact with daily.

However, Western society focuses its efforts on building one's own castle; self-sufficiency is the name of the game in Western cultures.

I was investing $250 million in building international logistics parks on the outskirts of some of Africa's largest cities. Knowing that community plays a central role in the cultures of Africa, I proactively met with and built friendships with the local communities, inviting them to the groundbreaking ceremony, explaining and giving tours of what we were building, and hiring some of them to work in our facilities.

Our investment was seen as an investment in the community. It was important to them too that our investment was successful. When we had to put a hold on construction due to the pandemic, we knew our investment was safe. The community was our eyes and ears on the ground, protecting and thus de-risking our $250 million investment.

Wealth as something holistic versus materialistic

In African cultures, wealth is something holistic. Whether in the form of cattle, crops, money, or wisdom, wealth is expected to be used to benefit the entire community. In Kenya, in the Swahili language, this is called *harambee*, meaning "Let's pull together." Whenever there is a need, Kenyans draw upon their community to raise funds for important local projects or to help somebody get the medical care they need.

In Western cultures, however, wealth — money, possessions, homes, cars — is predominantly seen as the possession of the individual who worked hard to earn it. What they earn is for them, to be spent on themselves as they see fit.

Let's take this notion of wealth one step further. The French sociologist Pierre Bourdieu identified three different types of wealth:[6, 7] economic capital, social capital, and cultural capital. Each one influences social order and power. Each type of capital also creates a different approach to and type of resilience and affects how countries deal with shocks and disasters.

---

6. Bourdieu, P. (1986). The forms of capital. In Richardson, J. (Ed.), *Handbook of Theory and Research for the Sociology of Education*. Westport, CT: Greenwood Press.

7. Bourdieu, P., & Thompson, J. B. (1991). *Language and Symbolic Power*. Cambridge, MA: Harvard University Press.

- Countries with a culture strong in social capital have populations who are willing and able to make the small or large personal sacrifices necessary to stop a disease or respond to a disaster.

- Cultural capital either creates a mindset of community and sharing of resources or a mindset of individualism and hoarding of resources for one's self.

- In countries with plentiful economic capital (e.g., cash, assets, and infrastructure), an expectation is generated that the powers that be will ensure the well-being of everyone. When people feel that their needs aren't being met, anger and protests result.

Western countries have deep pockets of economic capital and tend to rely on it to address shocks and challenges. African nations aren't blessed with such deep pockets but do have a natural propensity toward social and cultural capital, which leads to communities willing and accustomed to making sacrifices to help one another.

How can Western companies merge or marry their corporate culture and capital with the local culture and capital in order to create successful and resilient growth opportunities? By understanding what is important in the country they are expanding into.

Let's revisit the example of the international logistics parks. As an investor, we brought the economic capital to build the logistics parks that were not available locally. However, rather than lording it over them or acting arrogantly, we recognized that working hand-in-hand with the local community and respecting their culture would create a win-win for both of us. This made us both more resilient.

We were able to offer economic capital in the form of jobs, income, and improved infrastructure to the local community. They welcomed us into their community, offering us the social capital of a close-knit community that looked out for one another. By sharing our resources, we learned about and respected one another, and we created new forms of cultural capital that both grew our bottom line as a company and improved their lives as a community.

TAKEAWAYS

When the German and Indian foreign exchange students ran out of my high school classroom as the earthquake hit, it didn't mean they were not resilient. Their cultures — the context within which they had grown up — made them resilient in a different manner, one that was appropriate to their lives.

My Indian school friend was resilient to super spicy food that made my eyes water and throat burn when I ate it. My German school friend was resilient to temperatures below freezing and walking to school in the snow — both of which made me, a California girl, shudder.

Making the time and effort to understand local culture and context is the difference between companies that succeed and companies that fail when entering new markets; it is this awareness that makes companies truly resilient. This is more than a brief discussion or a cursory internet search. This requires having the appetite and willingness to create the bandwidth for your team to invest the necessary time (and budget) to get to know the realities on the ground prior to entering new markets. Only with this appetite and bandwidth will you know where and how to correctly invest your capital and develop your resilience.

For more information regarding our authors,
please visit bestsellerpublishing.org/2023anthology!

About Tom Wall, PhD, MBA, MSFS, CLU, ChFC

The best-selling author Tom Wall is a financial industry veteran with 20 years of experience and a PhD in retirement income planning. He has given keynote speeches to thousands of advisors from different backgrounds. He has spent most of his career as a product and strategy expert for a Fortune 100 company.

Early in his career, Tom experienced the devastating premature loss of his mother. With the subsequent loss of other loved ones, it became clear to Tom that we can't take it with us. So much was left on their tables, and Tom was led to conduct exhaustive research on how to help clients balance the spending and enjoyment of their money against saving for the future.

The surprising outcome was a focus on centuries-old strategies, many of which became much more attractive in 2022 due to an act of Congress. These strategies remain some of the best-kept secrets in the industry, and Tom has emerged as one of the foremost experts in this space. Today, he hosts a study group for emerging top advisors, produces thought leadership for the industry, and partners with advisors to drive client success.

For more information regarding our authors,
please visit bestsellerpublishing.org/2023anthology!

CHAPTER 16:

PERMISSION TO SPEND

BY TOM WALL, PHD

I was 24 years old when we got the news: my mother had cancer, and it had already spread throughout her body. The words were surreal, and the diagnosis was terminal. It was quite likely too late. But we all kept our chins up — most of all my mother, who turned out to be a stronger woman than I ever could have imagined. We knew there was always a chance, and that she'd fight as hard as she could.

It was March, and I was recently engaged, with plans to marry the following spring. Mom wasn't supposed to make it that long, so we moved the wedding to August. Over the next several months, I watched my mother struggle through treatments and everything that comes when you're fighting for your life. I would occasionally drive her to the hospital and run errands when needed — thrilled to fractionally repay her for all she'd done for me over the course of my life.

In the process, we had discussions like never before and became closer than ever. We were never much of a touchy-feely family, but we all started to say "I love you" and hug more frequently. The clock was our enemy, but in this amazing way, it was also our friend. It shaped my future relationships with my father, sister, and extended family. I was able to dance with my mother at my wedding and make memories over the subsequent holiday season that I'll never forget.

Shortly after that, about a year after she first got her diagnosis, I had the hardest night of my life as I held my mother's hand and experienced her passing away at the age of 54. She missed out on what was to have been an amazing, affluent, world-traveling retirement with her high school sweetheart — a hard-earned reward for decades of work, business travel, saving, and sacrifice.

At the time all of this was happening, I was a young financial advisor trying my hardest to make it in a very difficult industry. I was focused on learning as fast as I could, quickly obtaining advanced licenses and credentials to prove I knew what I was talking about. I was taught all the rules of thumb and basic principles to accumulate wealth and insure against the tragedies that can derail those plans. I was also taught how to ask great questions and uncover the hopes and dreams of my clients. However, one thing began to bother me, and I carried that with me throughout the rest of my career.

All these assumptions, best practices, rules of thumb, and tips for accumulating wealth rested on the expectation of a long retirement. They also maximized enjoyment of money in our later years, often requiring great sacrifice along the way. To me this seemed unfair, inefficient, and risky because you might not actually make it. And even if you did, you might not be physically able to enjoy it the way you could at a younger age.

While most healthy retirees will live into their 80s and beyond, many will not. If these folks have deferred enjoyment of that wealth their entire lives, then it could go to waste. As a smart guy who loves puzzles, I turned my focus toward figuring out how to maximize one's ability to spend at younger, healthier ages, while still following the fundamentals of financial planning.

YOU WILL BE AFRAID TO SPEND

No matter who you are, you most likely don't have an answer to the following question: When you arrive at retirement's doorstep with whatever sum of money you were able to accumulate, how much of it will you be able to spend each year? Put differently, you probably only have an accumulation strategy. What's your spending strategy?

Millions of Americans are under-enjoying their retirements right now because they're afraid to spend. They're afraid of what will happen if they outlive their assets. They're afraid of what will happen if they require expensive ongoing medical care — care that can quickly cost hundreds of thousands of dollars and isn't covered by any medical plan. They're afraid of what will happen if they need access to significant amounts of cash later in life for unforeseen circumstances. And those with children or strong ties to their community are concerned about the financial legacy they're leaving behind.

The bottom line is, they're worried about running out of money, and in response they are spending as little as possible, living well below the lifestyle their assets should be able to provide.

These people are victims of a generational shift that replaced pension plans with investment accounts, which completely transferred the risks to the individual. And they are woefully unaware of and unprepared for those risks, which is why they live scared and hoard money, just in case those unlikely risks become their reality. However, through a modern twist on a centuries-old product, one can confidently build a strategy to spend and enjoy that which has taken a lifetime to accumulate.

SAFE WITHDRAWAL RATES

Retirement income planning is actually a pretty new field. Historically, workers would go to work for a company that offered a pension in return for years of service. It was up to the company to make investments on behalf of the worker to ensure they could fund those promised benefits. Social Security would eventually help, and a retiree may have had other modest savings as well. If the mortgage was paid off by retirement, that could be enough.

In the 1980s, the country began shifting from defined-benefit pension plans toward defined-contribution 401(k) plans. Employee contributions to the plan shifted the burden for retirement saving to the employee. Employers have traditionally offered matching contributions, which is generally far less expensive than providing a pension.

But even with that shift, retirement planning wasn't historically all that difficult. When one could actually get reasonably high interest rates on certificates of deposit (CDs), savings bonds, and money market funds, retirees could invest their retirement funds in conservative vehicles and live off the interest. So long as they did not invade their principal, they were generally expected to be all right.

When rates began to fall below levels that would provide acceptable conservative investment income in retirement, some advisors started to study whether it might be prudent to take systematic income out of volatile investment portfolios — regardless of the interest rates or the returns they were earning. In 1994, an advisor by the name of William Bengen published a seminal study that led to what is commonly known as the 4% rule of retirement income.

Using stock, bond, and inflation data beginning in 1926, Bengen sought to determine what the maximum sustainable starting withdrawal rate was for each year, assuming retirement lasted 30 years. He dubbed this rate the SAFEMAX. It represents the highest amount someone could draw from a portfolio in their first year, after which they would adjust withdrawals for inflation.

In the worst-case scenario, an investor could start by taking just over 4% of the initial account balance. My own research in Figure 1.1 shows similar results, with key differences being a 60/40 stock/bond allocation and the inclusion of common investment fees, which an investor would pay in real life. What stands out is how different the results are when applied to various periods of time.

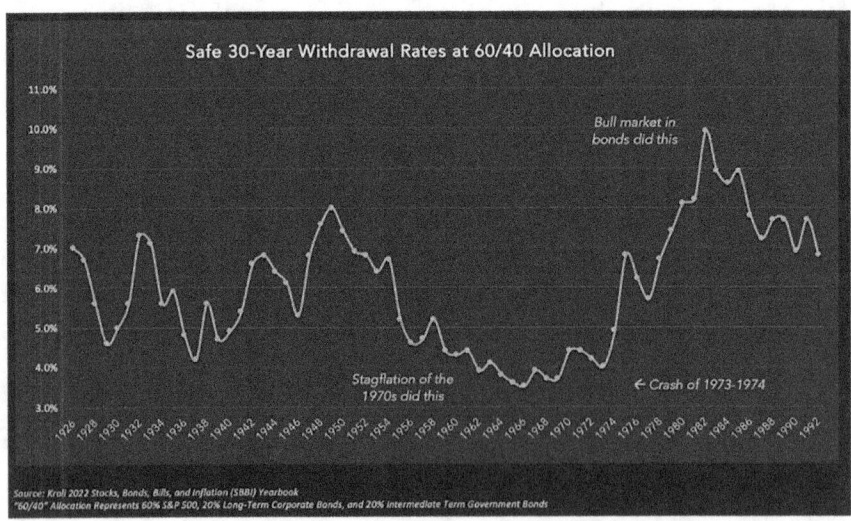

Figure 1.1: Safe 30-Year Initial Withdrawal Rates at 60/40 Allocation

An investor facing retirement has no clue what their future will end up looking like. History can only serve as a general guide of where to start, and each investor needs to check and adjust their spending at least annually to ensure they remain on track. That said, the two biggest threats to a safe withdrawal rate are subsequent investment returns and the need to inflate income.

Many studies have shown that, increasingly so for affluent retirees, the need for inflation-adjusted income is less important than previously assumed. In the early years of retirement and while still young, retirees are more likely to travel, dine at restaurants, participate in recreational activities like golf or skiing, belong to clubs, drive new cars, and so on. As people age, this discretionary spending tends to decline as their lifestyles contract. Thus, while nobody can escape the damaging impacts of market turmoil, wealthier clients with more discretionary spending are unlikely to be as affected by inflationary environments.

SEQUENCE OF RETURNS RISK

In retirement, staying the course may not always be possible because of the need for income. If your primary source of income is your investment portfolio and the market goes down, you have no choice but to sell a portion of your portfolio low and effectively make that year's negative return even worse. Furthermore, when your portfolio has a depressed value, the same level of income now represents a greater percentage of it, exacerbating the issue.

It can be quite difficult to recover from this. For this reason, average returns in retirement don't matter as much as the *sequence of returns*. To illustrate, consider the following example (Figure 1.2). Over the last 22 years, even with two of the largest stock market declines in history, aggressive investors with a hypothetical 80/20 portfolio experienced an average annual return of 8.54%.

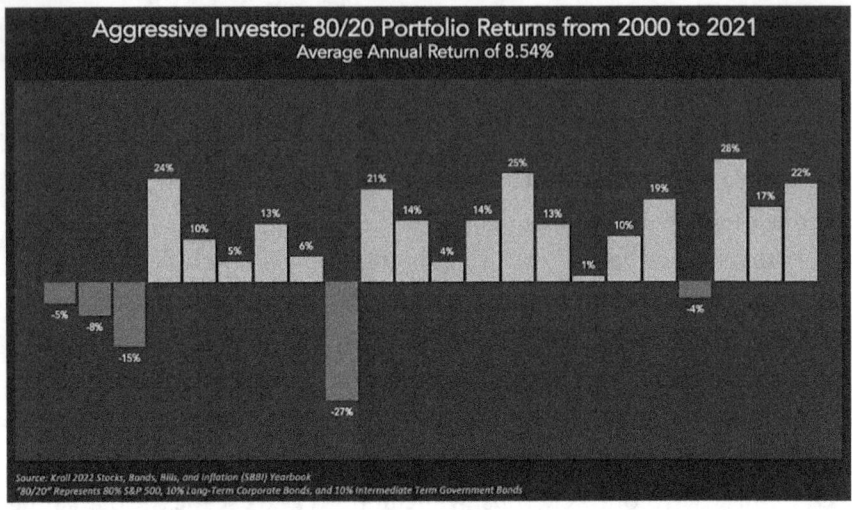

Figure 1.2: Hypothetical 80/20 Portfolio Annual Returns (2000–2021)

If someone considers taking a 6% initial withdrawal rate during a period that averaged 8.54%, they might assume that they would be safe and would still be making money during that period. However, experiencing negative returns early in that period and then compounding those losses by taking income would create an even worse environment that would become impossible to dig out of.

Even though the latter half of this return pattern was historically strong, it was too little too late. In the example in Figure 1.3, a retiree starting with $2,000,000 and withdrawing $120,000 per year would be left with only $159,593. This retiree, likely in their 80s at that point, would be one market crash away from running out of money.

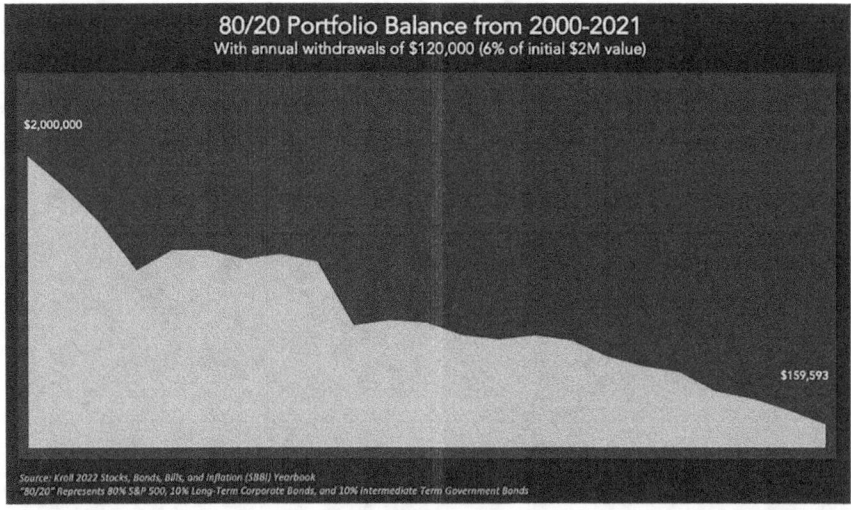

Figure 1.3: Account Value after Income (2000–2021)

But what if this investor had the exact same return in a different order? In the following example (Figure 1.4), the returns are exactly the same but arranged in reverse, with the large negative events occurring at the end.

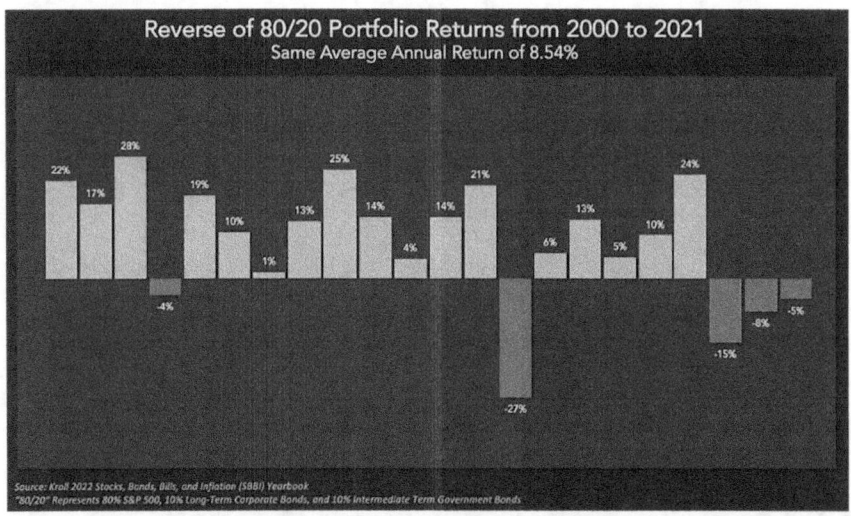

Figure 1.4: Hypothetical 80/20 Portfolio Annual Returns (2000–2021), Reverse Order

If that same retiree started with the same initial balance, the same withdrawal rate, and the same average return, how might the different order of returns have impacted the results? As you can see below (Figure 1.5 and Figure 1.6), the difference is staggering, with the retiree ending up with three times their initial balance, even after taking all that income.

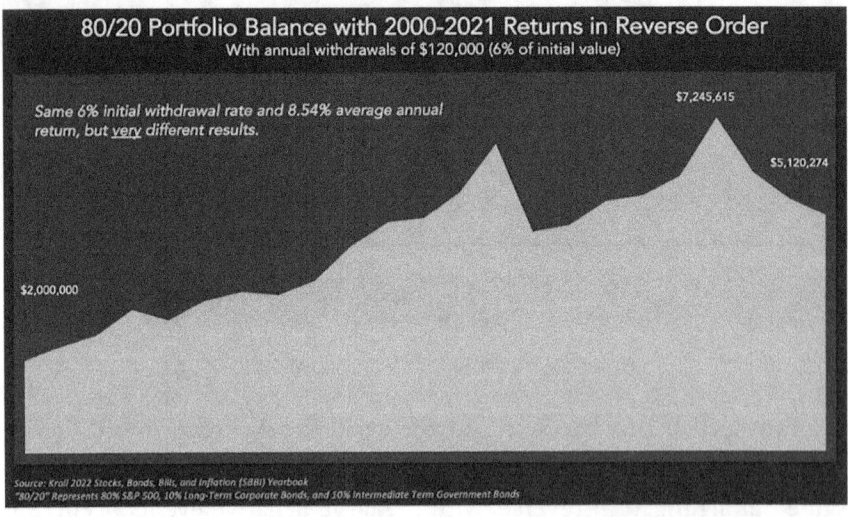

Figure 1.5: Account Value after Income (2000–2021, Returns in Reverse Order)

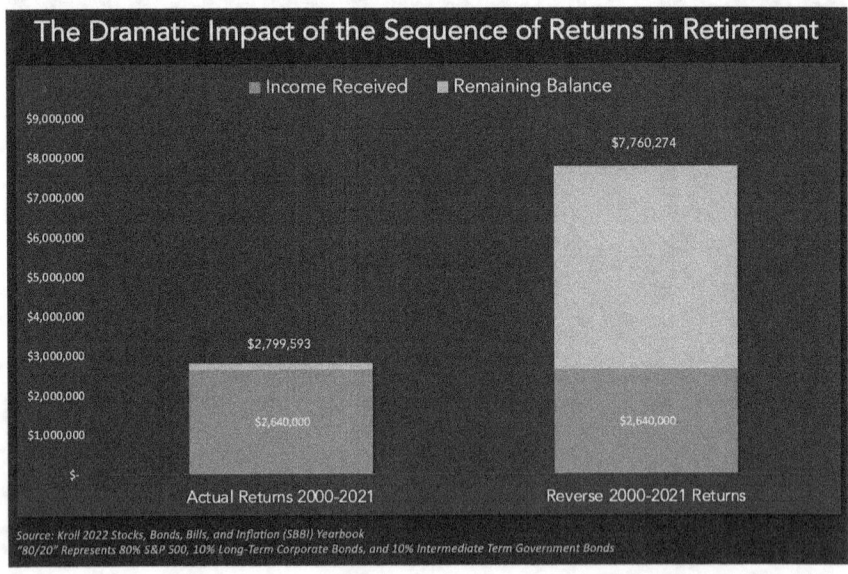

Figure 1.6: Impact of the Sequence of Returns when Taking Income

Timing is everything. Pure luck can be the difference between financial ruin and substantial wealth. This concept is meant to illustrate why it's imperative to diversify sources of income in retirement and not have all your eggs in one basket, so you're not forced to sell when times get tough.

THE BEST-KEPT SECRET IN PERSONAL FINANCE

The solution to the scenario above is to have other sources of income or to mitigate risks so one can more comfortably sell investments for income. There is one unique asset that I discovered early in my career — dividend-paying whole-life insurance — that allows one to predictably grow their wealth without risk, avoid income taxes while they do so, and have access to those funds at any time, even before retirement. These plans also typically guarantee a legacy to the next generation through death benefits that far exceed the policy cash values, and many also make those funds available to the retiree if they require expensive ongoing health care that isn't covered by traditional insurance or Medicare.

After working with thousands of advisors over the course of my 20-year career, I can confidently say that only a select few truly understand how to integrate these plans into a diversified investment portfolio.

About Nichole Lewis

Nichole Lewis bought her home at 22 and her first investment property at 23. Within 10 years, she had made millions in property. Now, with over 20 years' experience in real estate, she helps people replace their corporate salaries with passive income in 10 years or less, no matter where they're starting from.

Nichole, a full-time property investor and recipient of property awards for her ability to generate incredible property deals, is known as the Queen of Property. With a background working within global corporations as a speaker and mentor, Nichole created the Property Quadrants concept to revolutionize what real estate can do for you.

For more information regarding our authors,
please visit bestsellerpublishing.org/2023anthology!

CHAPTER 17

FINANCIAL RESILIENCE: BUY RIGHT
(FREEDOM FOUND THROUGH THE FOUR PROPERTY QUADRANTS)

BY NICHOLE LEWIS

The concept of Property Quadrants came from me reading Robert Kiyosaki's writing about cash flow quadrants. I thought to myself that it was highly relevant to real estate investing. I've been a professional real estate investor for 20 years now. I've made millions, I've lost millions, and I've had to start all over again.

I've made many mistakes on my path to millions, because I had nobody to teach me. I had to do things the hard way through trial and error. I was unfortunate enough to go through the global financial crisis with my first property down cycle, and that certainly brought me crashing down with a huge thud. The good news is, Property Quadrants has come from all of the things I've done well and all of the things I've done wrong, now making it easy for you to secure your financial future through passive real estate investing. Let me explain.

What prevents people from investing in real estate? We sent a questionnaire to around 1,000 of our clients to ask them what was keeping them from moving further ahead with their real estate investing endeavors. Interestingly enough, the answers that came back all boiled down to the same three problems — all of which are, in fact, myths and very easy to overcome.

1. People didn't think they could do property because they didn't have enough time to put into doing it well.

2. They thought it was far too risky because they didn't have the money to buy hundreds of thousands of dollars' worth of real estate.

3. They simply had no idea what to do next or where to start, due to a lack of knowledge.

I was amazed that it could all be boiled down so simply. Again, this was based on 1,000 clients, and the above is really where their concerns seemed to lie. These three perceived problems are very simple to overcome when you apply the Property Quadrants solutions. I'm going to take you through this, one quadrant at a time.

WHERE IS THE MAGIC?
(THE FOUR PROPERTY QUADRANTS)

For the sake of this chapter, I've created an avatar couple, John and Jane. They are typical of not only the 1,000 clients I surveyed, but many more thousands of people across the world doubting they can actually achieve their dream lifestyle in real estate. In reality, property is very simple. Let me show you how.

Property Quadrants split your property investing into four simple boxes:

1. Emotional property

2. Cash poor

3. Cash rich

4. Passive income

Quadrant number one is emotional property, namely your family home. You've purchased the home you live in based on an emotional buy. You love the property, you love the area you live in, and so you should. You spend time relaxing when you walk through the doors, and you have set up the house the way you want it.

Quadrant two is the cash-poor quadrant. This is basically where people make mistakes, usually because they use emotion to buy their first rental property. And that emotional buy leads to cash having to come out of your hard-earned paycheck. So you have cash coming out of your paycheck to pay your mortgage on your family home in quadrant one and more cash coming out of your paycheck to top up your mortgage on your first investment in quadrant two. This is a mistake. It's not your fault, though, because you didn't know any different — neither did I when I bought my first quadrant-two mistake property. By the way, 98% of people make the mistake of buying in quadrant two, myself included, with my first (and second) investment property.

Quadrant three is cash-rich property. This introduces you to how you can actually work in property to make active income that you can use to pay for your lifestyle and the down payment on your investment property. The magic of quadrant three means you don't get stuck having to spend years saving from your paycheck or waiting years for the real estate market to go up to create equity in your family home, allowing you to borrow against it to buy an investment.

Quadrant four is where the lifestyle magic happens. This is all about passive-income property. I have put together a very specific four-step formula that I follow every single time I buy a passive property investment. Passive income means it puts money in your pocket from day one, making you cash rich. Let me show you how John and Jane used these quadrants to create a passive-income lifestyle.

A Risk-Free Flip?

John was a corporate worker. He had a great job with good benefits, earning over $100,000 a year. He had an office romance with Jane and fell in love. She also was in the corporate world, earning a slightly smaller salary but sharing a lot of those benefits. After they got married, they bought their family home, and then they decided to have their first baby. Even though that was wonderful and life looked like rainbows, the financial struggles started.

First of all, they had to drop one income, even though it was temporary, because Jane was on maternity leave. They certainly struggled to live off John's salary alone. Struggle allowed the stress to start to creep into their lives. They wanted a second child close to their first one, but they couldn't work out how they were going to afford it. All of this meant that their retirement was at risk. And they now started to be shackled by stress and struggle, which they didn't want in their life.

They knew real estate was the way forward, as their friends had created massive wealth and were retired due to property. While they wanted to get further into real estate, like many of our clients, they were scared. They didn't want to risk their family home. They didn't have hundreds of thousands of dollars to spare in the bank, and they certainly had no idea where to start. They had very limited time with a newborn baby and John working as many hours as possible to earn a bonus.

When I met them, they were astounded to learn about quadrants three and four, the cash-rich quadrants. Most people don't know they exist. The cash-rich quadrants are the answer to eliminate both the lack-of-money factor and the risk factor. The first thing you do is earn as you learn. This stage also helps you start with your knowledge. The best part is, you can spend as little time as ten minutes per day!

You're instantly ahead of the game, because most people don't realize you can earn as you learn. In my book *Property Quadrants*, I take you through very specific examples about how my clients do no-money deals to make money when they start out. This helps you become an expert in a particular niche and an expert in a particular property area of your choice. You've got zero risk because you're putting in $0, and you'll make in property what becomes small change, like $5,000, $10,000, or even $20,000 per deal. The best part is, you put no money in when you make "loose change" deals. From there, most people will make the natural progression to flipping property. I love flipping; it's one of my favorite things. I aim to make at least $100,000 per flip.

You won't make that when you first start out (John and Jane didn't), but you will make money. They made $20,000 on their first flip. It took them one month to do the work and two months to sell and close. Time-wise, they would go on site for around five hours per week to visit and watch the work in progress. Jane could take the baby and stay no longer than 30 minutes. Jane quickly saw that her hourly rate was adding up to more than John's, based on the profit made from each flip. When you use tradespeople to do the work for you and you just oversee them, you can carry on in your corporate job (or being a mom, as Jane was) and make $20,000 with some change on the side. Yes, you have to pay your taxes, but you still have to do that with your job.

When you get into flipping property, the exciting thing is that there actually are a huge number of tax breaks. Believe it or not, as an employee you pay the most amount of tax because you can't claim anything back. Once you start your own business — which quadrant three is by providing active income — you actually end up getting a lot of tax breaks that add to your income. Within 12 months of starting with no-money deals in real estate, John and Jane were in a position where they had enough money to make the down payment on their first investment property.

Then I taught them about quadrant four, the passive-income quadrant, where you look specifically for a property that has multiple income streams and perhaps needs cosmetic work, such as paint, carpets, and maybe a new bathroom or kitchen. This cosmetic work very quickly adds value to your property and puts money into your pocket because you can increase the rent. John and Jane, with their very first passive-income quadrant-four property, were putting $400 a month into their pockets. That's $400 a month of passive income after all expenses are paid — after they've paid the mortgage, after they've paid their taxes, after they've paid their insurance, and after they've put some money aside for maintenance. They quickly realized that in order to replace Jane's corporate salary, they would need to buy only three quadrant-four passive-income properties.

John and Jane were starting to actually look good to the bank as well, because they added value; therefore, they had more equity. They also had money coming in, over and above John's corporate salary. Within five years, John and Jane actually managed to replace both corporate salaries. Jane had her next child and decided she wanted to stay at home and look after the children. John loved his job and decided he wanted to carry on working. The key here is "wanted to work." So when the corporation he worked for went through a restructuring and his job was on the line — which unfortunately these days is not a case of IF that's going to happen, but WHEN — he had no stress at all, because he didn't need to work. He chose to work.

Their retirement was set because they have money rolling into their bank account every single week. And their property investments are growing in equity — in other words, there is money on paper as the value of their property goes up, and there is cash in the bank. Also, their cash flow increases as rental payments go up every year.

READY FOR YOUR NEW LIFESTYLE?

This is what Property Quadrants can do for you. You can actually alleviate all of your concerns about property; you can strike off all of the problems as myths. The exciting part about this is that quadrants three and four create a perpetual loop. You can continue to use quadrant three to make money for your lifestyle, and you make money for your next down payment. You don't have to leverage against existing property or your home, and you don't need to leverage funds or borrow the down payment — which just creates more stability for your future.

If you'd like to have a next step and fully understand these quadrants more, you can always buy my book, *Property Quadrants* on Amazon. You can jump onto my website for The Property Lifestyle and go to my free training to learn more (more information available on the Anthology Author Resource page). For those of you who are super serious about your future, I now offer Done with You Property Quadrants coaching, where I guarantee I can help you buy a property within six months, or I'll keep working with you for free until you do.

For more information regarding our authors,
please visit bestsellerpublishing.org/2023anthology!

ABOUT LORI POLEP

Lori Polep's exposure to continuous learning started at a very young age as she listened to her parents discuss business challenges and solutions in the businesses they owned. Lori didn't realize it as a child, but those discussions started a foundation of knowledge that many others may never experience.

Lori worked for IBM after earning her bachelor of science in business administration with a focus on finance. She knew technology was the future. When she returned to the family business, she was able to create huge opportunities for growth through technological advances. Coupled with her belief in continuous learning, continuous improvement, employee engagement, mentoring, and process improvement, Lori sustained growth, productivity, and efficiency for the company and its employees.

As vice president and chief information officer, and with a master of science in business management (communication technologies) from Rensselaer Polytechnic Institute, Lori possesses unique problem-solving and process improvement skills which have saved the company millions of dollars. Through teamwork, sales grew to the tune of $1.3 billion, and Lori's negotiation skills continually saved the company money when working with vendors and suppliers.

Today, as a strategic advisor, Lori helps companies create sustainable businesses that support employees and continual, profitable growth.

CHAPTER 18:

BUILDING FROM ZERO TO $1.3 BILLION
(OVER 120 YEARS OF CHANGE)

BY LORI POLEP

Resilience is the ability to overcome obstacles. It is the ability to recognize the need for change and become stronger through it. It is also a mindset. In our case, it was starting over in each generation.

I grew up in the wholesale candy and tobacco distribution business which evolved into being a full-service convenience store supplier, where we sold most of the products a convenience store needs.

My great-grandfather emigrated from Russia. Leaving the country that you know for the unknown, with hopes for a better future, is its own resilience. That is what the United States is built upon.

By 1898 my great-grandfather had two farms, the first form of distribution. He was also in the tobacco business, with a store in Boston. I assume that my grandfather went to work for a candy and tobacco distributor in western Massachusetts during the Depression, as he was in Springfield in 1930.

My father worked for that distribution company as a teenager. When World War II came, he enlisted. When he got out of the Army, he asked for a $15-a-week raise. They didn't give it to him. He responded by starting his own business in my grandfather's cellar with his $444 mustering-out pay. He would take orders, pack the orders, and deliver them himself.

My father loved technology. His love of technology, coupled with his hard work and dedication, helped to grow the business immensely. *He embraced change.*

I worked in the family businesses as a child, learning business as I grew up. Fast-forward to 1980, when I joined the business full-time after working for IBM. The business was worth $78 million in sales. Between 1980 and 1984, we implemented cutting-edge technologies, which helped get us bigger customers, and we added product lines based on these customers' needs, such as groceries. *We listened to our customers and grew because we implemented strategies to serve them.*

In 1984, when our sales were $200 million, we were bought by the Trade Development Corporation. They bought successful family-run distributors all over the country. Unfortunately, they went bankrupt in September 1986. We all still worked there. It was devastating to us.

The bank would only let us buy the assets if we took on the liabilities, so we started the business from scratch in November 1986. We knew that we would be successful. There was no question. I remember it as being one of the best times of my life as we, as a team, were focused on building this business back to and beyond what it had been. We had the foundation, and we had the drive.

To start, we reduced the number of items by at least half. We concentrated on our best-selling items. We rented out half of our 100,000-square-foot warehouse. We had 60 employees versus the 200 we had employed before the TDC went bankrupt.

We did what we had to do to start building a profitable business.

By taking these steps, we reduced the cost of our loans for inventory and decreased operating costs because we rented out half of the building. We reduced the cost of labor, workers' compensation, auto and health insurance, and so much more.

To be resilient, you need to let go of your ego and embrace change. You have to be focused on the outcome and let go of what is not working.

We did that over and over again.

One does not build resilience when everything goes according to plan. What do you do when the plan goes awry? Because it will sometimes, no matter how much you have planned and how much effort you have put in. That can be hard to take. Yet we do not become successful if we just stay in that place. We become successful when we look at what occurred and figure out what went wrong and what we could do next.

No Band-Aid-ing Allowed ... (Elements of Building Resilience)

Building a resilient business takes a can-do attitude, with focus and determination. It also takes the ability to listen and recognize that there are problems to be solved. It is an opportunity to do things better.

One of the most important facets of building resilience in your business is to listen to the people doing the job. They are on the front line, seeing what is happening. When you have an environment where the employees are listened to, they will tell you that something is going wrong, and they will help find a solution. When they are part of a team, they want that team to be successful.

When I heard about an issue, I would go to the person doing the work. I would listen to determine if it was a training issue, if it was a software or hardware issue, if there was a need for process improvement, or if it was a combination of all of them. Why is that important in building resilience? You have to solve the problems at the source; otherwise, you are just Band-Aid-ing them and not rectifying the issue. This causes a loss of efficiency and productivity and increases costs.

I was at our management meeting, which was a cross-functional meeting of all our departments. The issues with our dispatching system, MobileCast, were being discussed. It used the same software that UPS owned and used, which was software that operated in real time. The trucks were not getting the right information to make the deliveries, and the dispatcher could not see all of the information. I went to talk to the dispatcher to understand what the issues were.

Then I talked to UPS Logistics and found we needed a software and hardware upgrade. There was additional software available that would help with route management. We implemented that, along with retraining people. The software upgrade helped to reduce costs because we were able to manage deliveries more efficiently.

I also took the time to look at the phones that were used with the system. The cost of service was dropping, so I was surprised when the bill was $6,000 a month. I called Nextel in for a meeting. Nextel was the only phone service available to work with MobileCast at that time, so my negotiation ability was limited. I was able to get the bill dropped to $1,200 a month, and we received a $6,000 credit.

By being in that management meeting, I discovered that there was a problem that I would not have known about otherwise. I took the steps to correct it before it became a bigger issue.

Resilience is learning from your mistakes. When things are not attended to properly, they create greater costs for your company and create inefficiencies.

I put processes in place to ensure that the dispatching system was kept up to date and to review the phone bills monthly. We saved a lot of money by renegotiating the phone bills often.

Two additional keys to having a resilient business are concentrating on process improvement and continuous improvement.

- Process improvement is a big undertaking because you are making major changes that can impact multiple areas of the company and require greater planning, long transition times, and more training.

- Continuous improvement is small, incremental changes. Those are much easier to implement, and less time and training are required.

Both of these build a stronger company. Process improvement and continuous improvement should happen with a cross-functional team that includes a member from every department touched by these changes. This allows for greater success because of the communication among the team members.

Without continuous improvement, we would not have been able to pivot as well in 2020 when COVID shut down the nation. We were an "essential" business that had to operate.

Continuous improvement always looks to create a better environment or solution. Because of that, we were always aware of bottlenecks within the system. With computer systems, one must determine where that slowdown is within several areas of the system, which we considered systematically: phone and data lines, network switches and wiring, firewalls, the computers themselves, and more.

Consider all of these parts as if you are on a four-lane highway, yet part of how the system connects is a dirt road. No matter how fast your computer is, if you want to connect to the outside world, you have to have all of these parts performing at the same level — and they have to be able to handle your peak business hours. When your business is growing, it may mean that upgrades must occur in parts of the system before something is paid off. As all of this is expensive, you don't want to overbuy and create high fixed costs, but you need to be able to react quickly to change.

Because of business growth, we ran into bottlenecks. After putting in a new phone system sized for 30% more throughput than needed, we bought a company the month after we went live with the phone system that increased our phone usage by 30% — and more at peak hours. Customers don't like busy signals. The way we found the problem was with a team made up of IT, the phone vendor, and a few other decision makers. The phone vendor analyzed usage and found that we were having issues during our peak hours. All of the trunk (phone) lines coming into the system were overloaded.

We realized that the increase in business, and therefore phone calls, created the issue. Because so much today is software-driven versus hardware-driven, we were able to pay a small fee to increase the phone system's capabilities and rectify the issue within a few days.

Sometimes the bottleneck is not apparent. When we had an issue with what seemed to be the computers running slowly, we looked at all of the touchpoints. The data lines were fast enough. We had already replaced many computers throughout the buildings. The network and the network wires had recently been upgraded. Where was this happening?

The issue was with our firewall hardware. Not the place we would normally think of, yet it is part of the flow of data. Again, this issue was found by a cross-functional team that reviewed and eliminated each possible area where a problem could be. The firewall was replaced with a very powerful one, just a few months before COVID …

OBSTACLES VERSUS IMPROVEMENTS

As the pandemic of 2020 began, we had already been using Microsoft Teams to host meetings throughout our organization. When COVID created the issue of people needing to work from home, that technology was already in place. We really stepped into high gear to work out solutions for making it feasible to have office personnel work from home.

We immediately bought Chromebooks for everyone who didn't have a computer at home. Because we reacted that quickly, these computers were still in stock. Every computer had VPN (virtual private network) software that provided a secure connection from that computer to our main computer.

Had we not replaced the firewall hardware, the system would not have been able to handle the increased data going back and forth over the computer network.

As you can imagine, there were supply chain issues. We already had software in place to limit the quantities of a product that one customer could buy when supplies were limited. That was key, as we had over 5,000 customers who were all demanding the same products. The order entry program would automatically reduce the order quantity.

The warehouse personnel were continually sanitizing the warehouses, especially the picking lines.

All of this happened quickly and efficiently because of the communication within and between departments.

Cross-functional teams provide knowledge of their areas of the company. Better solutions are created because of input from them. Problems are solved faster because of different ways of looking at an issue.

Continuous improvement keeps the company at its peak capability. Small steps increase the company's productivity and efficiency without major changes or influx of capital and build a stronger foundation.

The ability to see a problem and resolve it quickly is all part of continuous improvement and communication within and between departments. It is having a mindset that sees opportunities for improvement versus obstacles.

Resilience was built into the way we conducted our day-to-day business, which gave us the ability to pivot quickly. Cross-functional teams, continuous improvement, process improvement, and problem determination/resolution are all major parts of resilience, as is your mindset. Continuously building a stronger foundation gets you through tough times.

★ ★ ★ ★ ★

About Dr. Vladimir Frias

Dr. Vladimir Frias (DDS, MS, FACP) received his doctor of dental surgery and master of science degrees from Columbia University and completed a residency in prosthodontics at the Columbia Presbyterian Medical Center — followed by fellowships in maxillofacial prosthetics at the Bronx VA and the Nobel Biocare implant fellowship at the New York Presbyterian Hospital. He is a fellow of the American College of Prosthodontists, the American Academy of Maxillofacial Prosthetics, and a diplomate of the American Board of Prosthodontics.

Dr. Frias has been widely published, both in scientific literature and in his best-selling fictional Portia Black series. He is currently the chief of maxillofacial prosthetics at the Roswell Park Comprehensive Cancer Center in Buffalo, where he practices the full scope of surgical and reconstructive implantology, including craniofacial implants and anaplastology.

For more information regarding our authors,
please visit bestsellerpublishing.org/2023anthology!

CHAPTER 19:

THE EXPIRATION DATE
(THERE'S ONLY ONE WAY TO OUTLIVE YOUR BODY)

BY DR. VLADIMIR (VAL) FRIAS

I remember Beck every time I walk through the grocery store. I remember her every time I open a refrigerator, inspect a carton of milk, or turn over a can that's been sitting in the pantry too long.

"No expiration date," Beck had once tried to tell me, her voice destroyed by a tennis ball-sized melanoma that had grown from deep within the lining of her eyeball and spread its tentacles across her face. The resection to combat it had taken her right eye and most of her nose, tunneling through her maxillary sinus into her soft palate. Through the depths of that tunnel I saw her tongue struggle valiantly, squeezing itself into every crevice to squeeze out the words.

"No expiration date." It was a series of hisses, the air escaping from her eye socket instead of her mouth. She pulled out her phone, her fingers a blur on the keyboard: "I'm not a carton of milk," she typed. "My life has no expiration date."

TRUE TO FORM

Her name was Beck. Not Becky, Becca, or — God forbid — Rebecca. Beck. Like the musician. Artistic. Eclectic. Unexpected. Beck, who grew up on a dairy farm, showed 4-H beef at the state fair, and then turned vegan as a teen. Beck, who was a staunch pacifist with a virulent passion for mixed martial arts. She was smart, confident, witty, and occasionally abrasive, a girl who often had patience for everyone else but herself. She was the salutatorian of her high school class, who went to community college before transferring to a four-year school — because, in her father's words, she didn't want to be paying back loans at retirement.

And then 65 suddenly seemed so far away. She became Beck who, at 26, had just come from the palliative care clinic with an expiration date.

Three months after her initial diagnosis, she turned up at the maxillofacial clinic, often the final stop in the whirlwind of head and neck cancer care. It's a last-ditch chance at replacing the bits and pieces lost during multiple ablative surgeries. Plastic surgery attempts to replace the missing tissue with muscle and skin plucked from a forearm, then a thigh, eventually melted in the formidable beams of curative radiation therapy. The remainder of her tissue was left raw and untreatable by rounds of chemotherapeutics. Beck could have chosen to stay home with a bandage on her face but, true to form, she was not the kind to go out quietly.

The maxillofacial lab is a veritable Home Depot of 3D-printed nuts and bolts: silicone body parts in the shape of feet, breasts, eyes, and jaws. The drawers are stacked with boxes of titanium implants and abutments, fixation screws, and cadaver-derived bone and tissue grafts to hold them in place. The equipment is high-tech: face scans, 3D mills, photogrammetry, but the ultimate goals are not.

At best, the treatments we offer are a Band-Aid on a wound that will never close. My mentor once called it the spare-parts department, explaining every surgical procedure we performed in basic carpentry terms, and every prosthetic reconstruction we created as a plumbing job. Cut it, drill it, screw it back together and make sure it doesn't leak, spill, or regurgitate. Over the years, the standard white waste bins had been replaced with orange five-gallon buckets — the ones with the Homer character on the front: low-brim baseball cap, paint-stained apron, and oversized pencil.

People in the oncology business tend to use black humor to hide the fact that cancer care is often less cure, more crutch, and the myriad treatments can often be just as destructive to the human body as they are regenerative. Getting rid of cancer cells often means getting rid of the healthy cells that live among and around them, a carefully calculated risk assessment of how much collateral damage a person can take. An ablative surgeon I once knew referred to every hole he left as a parkway, depending on its size and tortuousness. Pelham, Saw Mill, Sprain Brook, Hutch. When he said he had a Taconic, the only parkway in New York State allowed to occasionally ferry buses, you knew trouble was coming down the pike.

Beck entered the room and removed her bandages with a flourish. "Taconic," she typed, "has nothing on me. You can drive an eighteen-wheeler through this." Gallows humor was something Beck gravitated toward. I believe she found it empowering, a moment of rare control in a spiral of chaos. Humor kept her going through the entire process.

Before she went under for her first surgery, she had held the operating room nurse's hand and asked which one of them wanted to be Thelma and which would be Louise. Her first surgery included an exenteration, a complete removal of her eye. In recovery she made a joke about staring death in the "eyes." Then she tapped on her screen and erased the "s." Before she went under for the surgery to implant the small titanium screws that would hold her prosthesis in place, she wrote, "I thought I got screwed a long time ago." Another time she scrawled, "I was whole. Now I am hole."

Once she had healed from her surgery, the arduous process of reconstruction began, with Beck scratching out questions and commands on her pad. There were the appointments to match her beau-blue eyes and cream-colored skin with pigmented swatches that could be replicated in acrylic and silicone. "What if I tan?" she asked. "What if Sephora stops carrying my favorite makeup?"

She never stopped thinking about the future. When we Spectromatched her skin for the pink and purple strands of flocking to match her irradiated skin, she pouted at the digital representation. "I knew I was just a number to you," she wrote.

We put her back together in pieces, the titanium abutments that connected to the implants buried under the grafted bone and skin, the samarium cobalt magnets that acted as the retention between that and a printed acrylic framework, the hand-painted ocular a representation of the missing eyeball. Finally, from a CT scan, a custom-milled plastic mold that would help replicate the parts of her missing eye, nose, jaw, and cheek in skin-colored, medical-grade silicone.

Beck called the process her Lego project. Arts and crafts day. She asked a young resident if he thought it was worth it to go to school for so many years to just mess around with Play-Doh. The resident laughed and told her she sounded just like his cranky 85-year-old grandmother. "Not 85," she wrote, "but I'm working on it." There was a lot of laughter, a burgeoning sense of relief. Things were going well.

Then, one day she turned up in a foul mood. She lashed out at the front desk, the nurses, and then at me. Halfway through the appointment she decided to get up and leave. I checked her notes, fresh in her records from her morning appointments. Her scans had come back positive. She was being referred out for a gamma knife.

Halfway through putting her back together, her lesion had recurred. The radiation was not curative; it was palliative. The expiration date had suddenly been moved up. I did what most of us do when our patients, our staff, and our families are not looking. I went home, locked the doors, drank myself into a stupor, and cried. The next morning I called her up and asked her what she wanted to do.

Her father told me, "She's not getting the radiation. But she wants to finish what she started." I didn't try to convince her otherwise. I set up her appointments. Two weeks later she had her prosthesis installed. A pair of large glasses hid the margins of the silicone where it touched the skin. A tint in the lenses attempted to hide the fact that her replacement eye would not move, that her lids would not blink.

I apologized for scientific breakthroughs that we hadn't been able to achieve yet. Animatronic eyes, silicone that would not depigment. I told her that one day we'd be growing her own tissue and suturing it into place, stem cell-derived human organs that, as of this day, are just lab meat in petri dishes, far from ready to be transplanted.

"I don't care what it looks like," she said. "I don't care what it feels like. I just need to be able to speak." And she could. With the hole in her face closed up, her tongue could approximate her reconstructed palate, and the hisses of air were now properly articulated words. I gave her a hug and made her a follow-up appointment. She never turned up.

A month later, Beck passed. I called, tried to tell her parents why I hadn't come to her funeral. I had a number of excuses ready, but the truth was, I wasn't sure I could make it through this one. I regretted saying that immediately. Half an hour of grief while she had suffered a lifetime sounded like such a cop-out. I was a coward, while she had been so fearless.

READY BEFORE EVERYONE ELSE

Close to a year later, her father asked to meet. He took out his phone and laid it on the table. On his voicemail list was one from Beck. The voice was sunny and bright, full of hope for the future. This was the Beck I had first met, before the surgeries, before the radiation, before the chemotherapy.

She began by thanking her family for a laundry list of things we take for granted on a daily basis. She thanked them first for the ice creams of the season, long rides on a lawnmower, trips to the lake. She thanked them for buying a trampoline even though her mother was sure she would destroy her face on it. She thanked her doctors and nurses.

She apologized for not following their instructions. She didn't take her pills, she ate and drank things she wasn't supposed to, she kept her prosthetic on at night. But she never once apologized for the way she would choose to live or die. After she had recorded that message, her father told me she had swallowed her hoarded pills and fallen into a deep sleep.

As her father left, we hugged and cried until he looked me in the eyes, his eyes as steely blue as Beck's. "Now stop this," he said. "Beck would be embarrassed for us." As he walked out the door, I stopped him.

"No expiration date," I said.

He looked at me quizzically.

"The voicemail," I said. "That's why she wanted to finish her treatment. She had something to say. Life has no expiration date."

Her father smiled. "She was ready for this," he said. "She was ready before everyone else."

Fourteen years of school, almost ten years of practice, and Beck had been ahead of me, of all of us, the entire way. In materials science, resilience is synonymous with toughness, the ability to bend without breaking. But Beck wasn't just adapting, she was creating.

For millennia, human beings have struggled with the idea of immortality: building, painting, writing, creating. The very idea of a tombstone is to outlast one's human body in inanimate form. And yet, as Beck had shown us, the only true way to outlive your body is to pass a little of yourself on to others. When people can hear you, you have no expiration date.

If you see me in a grocery store giving a milk carton a thumbs-up, know that I'm not crazy. Just know that I learned a lot about life from death. And when a magical soul like Beck comes through your life, don't forget to listen to what they have to say.

AFTERWORD

THE POWER OF REBOUNDING

BY MATTHEW D. SCHNARR,
BSP AUTHOR FULFILLMENT COACH

It has been such a pleasure and honor to work with each of the authors in this book — along with all of the authors at Rob Kosberg's Best Seller Publishing. I am forever grateful for being able to work with such fine examples of resilience. I often see industry leaders facing challenges and rebounding in miraculous ways, and I would like to share this sentiment in closing.

Through senior prom in high school, I knew there was one place that I wanted to work — indefinitely. As a drama kid, an avid fan of early cinema, and a teenager of faith desperate to catch up on secular films, there was only one place for my idle hands: the movie theater. With my driver's license and diploma around the corner — and absolutely no idea of where life would take me — the sizzle pop of soda and flickers of blockbuster eye candy beckoned me with a thick aroma of butter and carpet cleaner.

During my first year, I had my eyes on the same job most of the new hires wanted: film projectionist. My coworkers and I didn't know it at the time, but we would be the last to thread Technicolor through spikes and gears and knobs and light. Digital cinema would arrive with the Great Recession, the impact of which was also out of our foresight. Nevertheless, we wanted the extra cents per hour and the potential ability to invite friends to super-forbidden midnight showings.

After months of shoveling popcorn out of the kennel (and off the floor, as needed), I earned my shot. I can't deny hoping that this position came with admission to some secret society, but I was okay with mundanity. Reels of film were delivered to my trusted hands. Not only would I hold impressive flicks, but I also spliced trailers of splendor yet to come — all to be witnessed by enthusiastic attendees.

Unfortunately, the glory of my position also involved projectors that were quickly becoming out of date. The intricate, necessary parts that made up these machines were becoming rarer by the year, and I would quickly learn a brand-new term: brain wraps. If the projectionist missed a notch or twisted the film, or if something broke, the film could tie itself in a knot or wrap itself around the inner workings of the projector. If I was at the wrong place at the wrong time, the latest Pink Panther flick might just slip, slide, and loop itself around everything in sight.

With a great helping of gratitude, I can share with you that I was not responsible for any fires, pandemonium, or motion picture lawsuits. Thankfully, while brain wraps were unwanted, there was a process in place to deal with them. Scissors, a couple of tools, and tape were all that I needed to keep the show going on. Unfortunately, regardless of my skill and pace in responding, I was gaining a showstopper reputation — and not in a good, standing-ovation way. All too often, the movies I was in charge of halted, tore, and melted on-screen.

How I cringe to this day at my manager's displeasure. There may have been many reasons for my shortcomings. Maybe my training was too quick (but someone quit at the wrong time). Maybe the theater needed new projectors (but other investments were being made). Maybe I'm a bad luck magnet (but I refused to let that be the end of it). All that was known was that I was becoming a record holder — and this record wouldn't come with any awards.

Four weeks into my dream job, and it felt like I was about to lose everything. I had been summoned to the manager's office. My mind was filled with thoughts of no more soda. No more flickers. No more candy.

I dreaded my next shift, as I knew it could be my last — at least before returning to cleaning counters ...

SEVEN YEARS OF AUTHORITY

Nearly a decade after my movie theater days, and a couple of years after graduating from college with a Creative Writing degree, I started working with Rob Kosberg. Before meeting him, my humanities major seemed like an enjoyable yet narrow dead end. Thankfully, a college buddy connected me with Best Seller Publishing. Lo and behold, the curriculum behind my degree matched Rob's Enhanced Ghostwriting™ to a T.

I began as a freelance writer working on occasional book projects. I traded my scissors and tape for a keyboard and computer screen. Instead of the one-way street of cinema, I found myself on the two-way street of book creation, assisting a variety of experts through the various challenges of sharing their minds and experiences with the world. In entering the world of Authority Marketing, I traded brain wrap for writer's block.

After nearly three years, I heard Rob describe me to a room of experts as "vital to the process" during one of his seminars. For me, this was a great moment of affirmation and encouragement. I could not help but feel that I was a blessed man.

By this time, I had already learned so much from a selection of wonderful, modern leaders. In the harmony of so many different voices and the encouraging hum of their concepts collecting in my brain, I listened to experts who shared something far more than success and glory. Mistakes and grief revealed themselves to be a cruel but important thread throughout many backstories. Some of our authors shared these with their readers. And some shared them with me, behind the scenes, as we crafted their life experiences into colloquial wisdom.

Blessed. To this day, I definitely continue learning a lot working at Best Seller Publishing. And one of the most important lessons regards the challenges we inevitably encounter in each of our stories. We can learn from mentors, books, and media. We can learn from training and curricula. As we utilize what we learn, some of it might even stick due to routine, exposure, and autopilot. However, nothing sticks quite like the horror of making a mistake — or the resilience of pulling yourself together after a dark chapter of life.

I always heard the word "mentor" and understood its definition. But something clicked during my first seven years with Rob Kosberg. A mentor shares their mistakes. Yes, maybe they do this so that others can avoid similar outcomes. I think they also do this to provide reassurance that mistakes are inevitable — if not invaluable. A mentor also shares the mornings when they couldn't face a day — and how they found the courage to put some pants on and get to it. Again, reassurance can be found in knowing that, while challenges and loss await us, so do our moments of strength.

The lessons and courage we earn through mistakes and grief belong to us. We don't inherit or learn them from a teacher. And while we might cringe as we think back on an occurrence, someone once told me, "Cringes are great. They're a reminder of the last time you needed to learn that lesson." I like to think that as we cringe a little less, we can beam with a little more self-esteem.

Personally, these days, I grin often. Every day, I see progress as I witness my authors facing the challenges of writing their books. It's easier said than done (unless of course you're using speech to text, *ahem*). I see professionals pivoting and rebuilding on a daily basis, conquering time and emotions to reach their goals. They see me, too, and they encourage me. And so, I grin as I grow, affirming their truths in my own journey.

WELL AFTER PROM ...

So, back to the end of high school. I was dreading work the day after another dreaded brain wrap. Thankfully, I wasn't about to lose my job. However, a conversation needed to be had. My managers at the movie theater said they weren't very thrilled about the number of movies interrupted on my watch. But when the film snapped, I was there to tape it back together and get the reels spinning again. The incidents never got worse — they got solved. Beyond that, my team appreciated that I showed up to work on time with enthusiasm. They decided to be patient.

Everyone was still a little anxious about the pattern that had been forming until that day. Over the next few weeks, a new pattern emerged … there wasn't a projector problem that I couldn't solve! Even if I was off shift, watching a complimentary feature, chances were good that I'd be needed upstairs. Each projector had its own flaws and malfunctions. Due to my exposure to every possible brain wrap gone haywire, those defects were well known to me. I was now on my way to becoming Head Projectionist.

Eventually, I found myself pivoting to the DVD rental industry. When I submitted my two weeks' notice at the theater, I was told by our general manager that my track record would be well worth an extra dollar an hour to keep me on his team. That will forever be one of my favorite compliments. Nevertheless, it was on to the next chapter for me, wherever that might lead. After the recession, and after a couple of pages, the next chapter was college. And then a few more pages turned, and I found my place at Best Seller Publishing.

I will never forget those late nights at the theater, accepting the next big movie, splicing it together, and maybe testing the film out with coworkers (to ensure it was ready for weekend audiences, of course, *wink wink*). Looking at it now, it's no surprise that I would, years later, trade the projection room for late nights splicing transcripts together into manuscripts. Brain wraps, stories, lessons — I just needed some scissors and tape.

My experience at Best Seller Publishing amounted to an important landmark in 2021 when we published our *Wall Street Journal* best-selling anthology, *The Experts Cure: How Entrepreneurs Are Changing the World*. I found myself managing 20 authors. The COVID pandemic was still ongoing when we all got started together. And each of the authors had their own unique spark of optimism. Yet again, I was blessed. Every call involved came with unity. Every chapter I confirmed for the anthology added to and sustained the harmony of the amalgamating truths I would continue carrying with me.

Blessed. Entrepreneurs — by nature of facing the unknown and risking complete pivots — are an identity of resilience. Small business owners — by nature of carrying responsibility and encouraging potential — are bearers of resilience. And thought leaders — by nature of motivation, introspection, and vision — are builders of resilience. And I have the pleasure of helping all three share their stories.

Unfortunately, part of my professional life involves seeing these leaders face loss and tragedy outside of books and business. Since the COVID pandemic, we have witnessed more and more authors responding to the loss of friends and family. Maybe it isn't our designated service, but it's an honor that we can send some love in a time of grief, generate and sustain encouragement, and share some hope for the better days ahead. Given time and spirit, we always see them rise again.

As I reached the end of working on *Expert Resilience*, I was struck by how much resilience I see every year. As I improve personally and professionally, the universal truths our authors share crescendo with their successes and with my progress. As I face mistakes and failures, with much gratitude, I stand grinning with giants.

As you reach the end of our newest anthology, I hope you are doing well. No matter the cringe that might strike the forefront of your mind, I hope you remember that it was the last time you needed to learn that lesson. No matter the challenge in front of you, I hope you remember how bad you whupped the last rough workday that stared you down.

May you see your resilience, and may you pass it forward.

Blessed.

For more information regarding our authors,
please visit bestsellerpublishing.org/2023anthology!